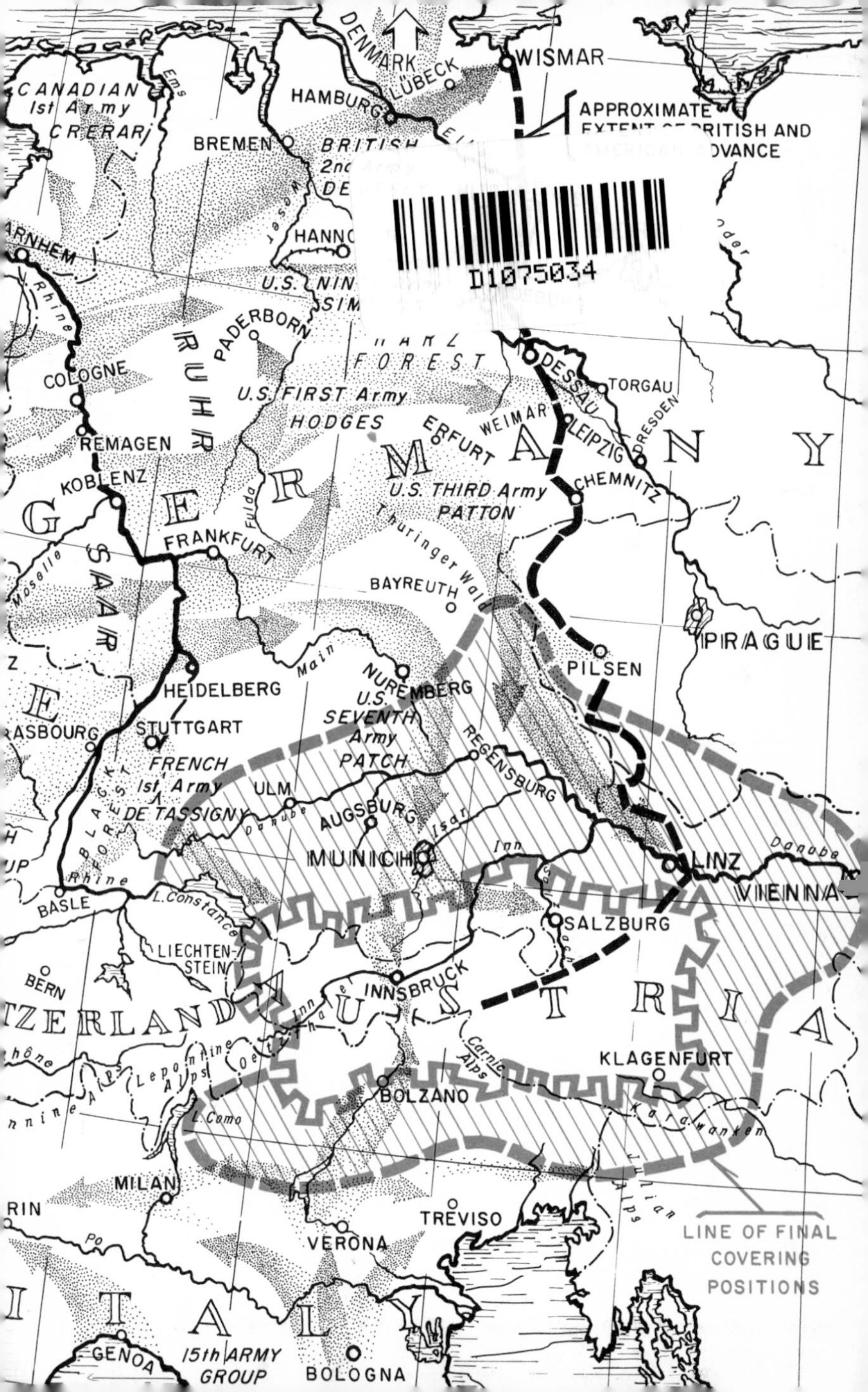
DENMARK
WISMAR
LÜBECK
HAMBURG
APPROXIMATE EXTENT OF BRITISH AND AMERICAN ADVANCE
CANADIAN 1st Army CRERAR
Ems
BREMEN
BRITISH 2nd Army DEMPSEY
Weser
HANNOVER
ARNHEM
Rhine
U.S. NINTH Army SIMPSON
Oder
PADERBORN
RUHR
HARZ FOREST
COLOGNE
U.S. FIRST Army HODGES
DESSAU
TORGAU
WEIMAR
LEIPZIG
DRESDEN
ERFURT
REMAGEN
G E R M A N Y
KOBLENZ
CHEMNITZ
U.S. THIRD Army PATTON
Fulda
Thuringer Wald
FRANKFURT
SAAR
Moselle
BAYREUTH
PRAGUE
PILSEN
Main
NUREMBERG
HEIDELBERG
STRASBOURG
STUTTGART
U.S. SEVENTH Army PATCH
REGENSBURG
FRENCH 1st Army DE TASSIGNY
ULM
BLACK FOREST
Danube
AUGSBURG
Isar
MUNICH
Inn
LINZ
VIENNA
Rhine
BASLE
L. Constance
SALZBURG
LIECHTENSTEIN
BERN
INNSBRUCK
SWITZERLAND
A U S T R I A
Inn Thal
Oetz Thal
Carnic Alps
KLAGENFURT
Rhône
Lepontine Alps
Pennine Alps
BOLZANO
Karawanken
L. Como
Julian Alps
MILAN
TREVISO
LINE OF FINAL COVERING POSITIONS
TURIN
Po
VERONA
I T A L Y
GENOA
15th ARMY GROUP
BOLOGNA

THE FORTRESS

THAT NEVER WAS

THE FORTRESS

THAT

The Myth of

NEVER WAS

Hitler's Bavarian Stronghold

by Rodney G. Minott

Holt, Rinehart and Winston

New York · Chicago · San Francisco

To P. K. M., with devotion

Preface

General Dwight D. Eisenhower once rather pointedly reminded me that war is not fought in a classroom. While the remark is hardly original, it nonetheless states a fundamental truth that confronts the historian and should be borne in mind. Eisenhower's strategy and tactics have been questioned by many of those who fought both for and against him. The Berlin problem and especially the Anglo-American failure to seize the city have caused contention. This book's purpose is not to serve up an exposé of "why we do not have Berlin today." It is rather an attempt to examine only one aspect of the European campaign's waning months and try to ascertain what part it played in determining Eisenhower's strategy and tactics. His main purpose, of course, was defeat of the German field forces; Berlin, a political pawn, became entwined with the various military factors.

The subject under examination is the history of the Nazi Alpine Redoubt and its strange hold upon various intelligence services. In recent years the Redoubt has been relegated to a form of military-historical limbo. Mention of it is made, but no true examination of its effect upon the last Western Allied campaign in Europe has ever been undertaken.

In 1944–1945, Eisenhower played the key part in fashioning the strategy for the subjugation of Nazi Germany. As Supreme Commander, he had under his control diverse armies totaling about four million men and women. One former British officer says that Eisenhower's duty was really not that of a Commander in Chief in the classical sense, but rather that of a Generalissimo or military statesman. His primary job was to keep an alliance together and few men have ever done such a task so well.

Maintaining an alliance means compromises and the bruising of national as well as of personal egos. This part of his command responsibilities during 1944–1945 must be remembered at all times. His strategy was constantly hobbled or circumscribed by the very nature of administering a military coalition. These factors are extremely important and when they are combined with the circumstances of Eisenhower's general lack of professional experience at that time, the burdens he carried are more easily understood. Furthermore, his inexperience was generally shared by both his American superiors and subordinates. At that point in Western history, power passed from the experienced but exhausted hands of Great Britain to the strong but impetuous ones of America.

In the wave of bloody history that swept the world in 1944–1945, this transference of power from one nation to another could be considered a major current, while the story of the Western Allied Command in Europe and the National Redoubt are attendant lesser ones. The last two were important and they may have helped determine to some degree the direction in which the wave went, but from the Free World's point of view, the major factors were Great Britain's unwilling but inevitable relinquishment of responsibility and American ingenuousness in the face of new duties. The Redoubt, then, is but a part of the historical tide in the last year of the war.

I have attempted to keep the focus of the book almost exclusively upon those events and personalities directly connected with Hitler's Alpine stronghold. Many persons, I am sure, will find areas within the story where they feel certain individuals or occurrences may have been slighted or ignored. I am cognizant of such limitations. The tale is, however, as balanced and accurate a one as I could fashion.

Every author, unless churlish, acknowledges the vast help given him in assembling material, providing criticism, and doing the manual labor of research and typing. The persons to whom I am most indebted are: Professors Thomas Bailey and Gordon Craig, both of Stanford; Professors Charles Burdick and Richard Cramer of San Jose State College, San Jose, California;

Professor Jon M. Bridgman of the University of Washington in Seattle, Washington; Professor Charles McLaughlin of the School of International Service, the American University, Washington, D.C.; and Professor W. Gerhard Burkhardt of the University of Hamburg. I owe thanks to the entire staff of the World War II Records Division, National Archives and Records Service, Alexandria, Virginia. This efficient group includes: Sherrod East, Director; Wilbur J. Nigh, Chief of the Reference Branch; and Mesdames Lois Aldridge, Caroline Moore, and Frances Rubright.

The Pentagon assisted in the procurement of photographs, and credit for this service is hereby given to Lieutenant Colonel Charles W. Burtyk, Jr., Chief, Magazine and Books Branch, Office of Information, Department of the Army, and to Miss Donna Traxler, Signal Corps, Department of the Army.

Finally, great appreciation must be expressed for the manuscript typing and research assistance provided by Miss Connie Sue Cook, University of Texas, and Miss Elizabeth Anne Moore, Stanford University.

—Rodney G. Minott
Stanford University

Introduction

Berlin. It must seem to most persons in the world, both East and West, that the former German capital has been a trouble spot for the better part of this century. Currently, she lies a hostage, with two powerful political blocs nervously contending for her. A bad miscalculation by either group could incinerate civilization. The story of how the city managed to find itself in its present circumstances is a very curious one. There are many highly complicated factors involved, but its roots go back to 1944 when the Western Allies prepared to invade Occupied France.

Grand strategists generally tend not to be too specific in outlining their objectives, for their concern is really policy-making. They define the general goals and subordinates figure out the specific means by which they are to be obtained. As an example, the

Western Combined Chiefs of Staff in 1944 simply directed the Allied Supreme Commander, Dwight D. Eisenhower, to drive into Germany's heart and destroy her field forces. The details of how this was to be accomplished were left to Eisenhower, his immediate staff, and his subordinate commanders. Eisenhower, in turn, mapped out a more specific strategy for his forces, and his army commanders devised the campaign tactics that achieved success.[1]

The theory, however, was less complex than the practice. Coalition warfare is the most difficult type to organize and direct. Eisenhower and his Chief of Staff, Lieutenant General Walter Bedell Smith, decided that the industrial heart of Germany was the Ruhr. Capture the Ruhr and Germany's most vital war-making organ would be denied her. A logical direction in which to move after seizing the Ruhr was toward the German capital, Berlin, in the northeastern part of the nation.

The original Allied strategy called for an advance upon the Rhine River with the main thrust to the north, following the European coast. This was thought to be the most desirable of plans because the terrain to the north near the Rhine favored the mechanized type of war waged by the Americans and British. Such an attack, essentially a single-thrust one, would isolate the Ruhr from the rest of Germany most expeditiously, and also, Northwestern Europe's finest port, Antwerp, would lie in the path of the armies. If Antwerp could be captured, communication and supply lines would be materially shortened. The general idea was to destroy as many German units as possible west of the Rhine, cross the river, and press on, giving priority to the northern flank of the Allied drive which would be predominately British. If the attack was a success, the Ruhr would be cut off and the victorious British and Americans would then drive hard in a northeasterly direction toward Berlin.

By mid-September, 1944, the Supreme Commander re-evaluated his strategy. He still intended to wrest the Ruhr from enemy control, but he was not quite so sure about Berlin. He felt that his advancing troops might be held up on the Elbe River, and that it was entirely possible for the Russians to reach Berlin first, due to the success of their mighty 1944 summer offensives. As a result of this modification of his original views he suggested to his subordinates that while Berlin was still the major goal, future operations should be undertaken in concert with the Russians. He advised his army group commanders that instead of a concentrated Allied drive on Berlin, the British Twenty-first Army Group, under Field Marshal Sir Bernard L. Montgomery, might seize the northernmost provinces of Germany with their North Sea and Baltic Sea ports, while the American Twelfth Army Group, under General Omar N. Bradley, should capture the central Leipzig-Dresden area, and the American Sixth Army Group, commanded by General Jacob L. Devers, should occupy the southern Augsburg-Munich sector. The British commander, Montgomery, however, wished for a continuance of the single drive in the north to be undertaken primarily by his army group, buttressed by an additional American army under his command.[2]

By the end of December, 1944, however, the situation had changed. The Russian eastern offensives had ceased and there was every chance that their armies might not take Berlin for months. No one was sure of their intentions. The American Ninth Army had been assigned to the British Twenty-first Army Group as a result of the bloodily intense Ardennes campaign. Confusion attended the subsequent role of the Ninth Army, commanded by Lieutenant General William H. Simpson; there was doubt about how it was to be employed in connection with the Allied strategy for the war's final drive. Apparently, the British felt that they were to retain the American army and, with this added power-punch, make the final campaign an assault aimed in Berlin's direction. Perhaps Eisenhower intended that such a move be made, but the evidence is not entirely clear. In any case, after the Ninth Army Group seized the Remagen bridgehead on the banks of the Rhine on March 7, 1945, Eisenhower decided to shift the axis of the Western Allied attack from the north, with Berlin as a possible goal, to the south.[3]

The reason for Eisenhower's swinging the balance of his attack away from the north has aroused intense and, at times, bitter speculation, since many feel it delivered Berlin (and eventually Prague) into the hands of the Russians. There were many reasons given for the shift, but one of the major considerations offered by Eisenhower, as well as by his Chief of Staff, Bedell Smith, and by the Twelfth Army Group's Commander, Omar Bradley, was concern over a Nazi last-ditch stand in an area that comprised the mountainous parts of Bavaria, Austria, and Northern Italy. It was approximately 240 miles from west to east and 80 miles from north to south. This alleged center of fanatical resistance carried such titles as "the Southern Redoubt," the *Alpenfestung* (Alpine fortress), "the Bavarian Redoubt," or "the Inner Fortress," but among the Allies, it was most familiarly known as the "National Redoubt."* Its story is an interesting one, for in truth, the Redoubt never truly existed save in the minds of some Nazis, a very few German generals, and perhaps too many American officers. Unhappily, for the Americans, they inadvertently created the myth and were forced to live with it.[4]

The Redoubt, in the estimation of General Omar Bradley, shaped the tactical thinking of the Western Allies in the closing weeks of the war in Europe. Indeed, he refers to the concern over the Redoubt as an "obsession." It was not universal by any manner of means, but the question is: How could so many highly intelligent and hardheaded soldiers make such a mistaken evaluation of a fortress system that never was? The fault does not lie solely with the Supreme Headquarters, Allied Command (SHAEF). An examination of the Redoubt's history shows that the Germans and

* The author has used the terms "Redoubt," "National Redoubt," and *Alpenfestung* interchangeably throughout the book.

the Russians as well as the Americans were highly confused about its existence. Only the British seem, generally, to have had a pervading skepticism about the Alpine fortress. The story holds some relevant lessons for us today and so may be studied with profit.[5]

The End and

The Beginning

Part 1

1

Nothing made much sense. It was early May, 1945, in West Central Europe and the war was almost over. Depending upon who one was and where he was, certain oddities distorted the image of immediate victory or defeat.

To soldiers of the American Seventh Army, pushing south from Munich toward Innsbruck, aiming for the Brenner Pass, or in the United States Third Army farther east, driving down on Linz, the war was almost bearable. The weather was pleasant most of the time. Throughout Bavaria and in Austria the enemy citizens sometimes applauded and pressed wine upon the GI's. It was received with martial appreciation— as the conqueror's due. Many of the towns were "tattletale gray"; a variety of bedsheets and similar articles were hastily flung out of windows by the inhabitants to prove to the invaders that within the buildings dwelt the most pacific of peoples.

This was decidedly odd. According to rumors and intelligence briefings, the troops, especially those in the Seventh Army, were piling through the center of what was alleged to be a fearsome fortress system. If there were not fanatically manned strong points to be encountered, there would at least be guerrilla activities among the citizenry. The fanatics, however, must have been elsewhere. And if the civilians had deep-laid plans for subversion, terror, and sabotage, they successfully managed to camouflage them under a variety of moods that ranged from bewildered apathy to some form of elation at the war's impending end. All units of both armies rolled on, fanning out over Southern Bavaria, Western and Central Austria.

Being a member of the German army in that geographic area at that time presented its own problems. In the path of the American Seventh Army's advances, the German soldiery not only found themselves militarily overwhelmed, but they also discovered that their civilian countrymen preferred not to associate with them. Hiding on the hillsides or within copses and behind hedges, they watched with sullen envy as the citizens dispensed their spirituous liquor to the victors. If the defeated troops were lucky, they got water. Also, most of the Americans seemed to be motorized and to have inexhaustible supplies of practically everything needful.

In disgust, many of the German soldiers came out and gave up the fight. The war was as good as over

4

anyway and the Americans treated them decently. They simply waved their captives to the rear with a minimum of security arrangements and the people tried to be indifferent. Yes, American captivity was infinitely preferable to falling into Soviet hands, and if the senseless fighting went on, there would be a chance of the latter. The Russians were driving up from Eastern Austria and who knew what might happen? Things were peculiar in defeat. Germans had even fought Germans in Munich and there were similar tales elsewhere.[1]

It may have been spring in Southern Germany and Austria, but it still was almost winter to the Americans of the Eighty-eighth Infantry Division crunching northward through the Dolomite Alps from Italy. These men were attached to the Fifth Army of the Mediterranean-based Allied Forces Headquarters. Their object too was the Brenner Pass and a union with the troops from the European front. It snowed and winter equipment, including shoepacs, was issued. May in the Alps, at least on the Italian side, was a freezing and too-familiar experience to these Americans.[2]

Then on May 2, five days prior to all other German fronts, the Italian sector unconditionally surrendered. The Americans of the Eighty-eighth Infantry Division, who were leading the advance, learned of the capitulation from their adversaries, of all people. It was hard knowledge to come by from the GI's point of view, because the news was delivered into the American lines by some old enemies—the German First Paratroop Division. The paratroopers informed the Americans that the war was over in Italy and all units—United States and German—were ordered to hold their present positions. The Americans, unable to get confirmation from their own headquarters, feared a trick.

A regimental colonel ordered the Germans in his vicinity to surrender within one hour. A second German party, trying vainly to convince the infantrymen of the surrender, were also ordered to capitulate. The German paratroopers threatened to fight if the Americans advanced. A short, nasty and completely useless fight broke out, resulting in ten American casualties. Since the terrain was so mountainous and the infantrymen so strung out, it was twelve hours after the war in Italy was over before general combat ceased.[3]

By the time the GI's in the forward elements gathered what had happened, everyone else seemed to know that the Italian fighting was over. When it was official, though, the troops were doubly thankful. They had had a miserable war fighting in the Italian Appenines, and they had received scant attention from home after the spectacular landings in the west. The Dolomite Alps were the highest in Italy; and when the word came for the troops to move up into them, there was a sense of gloom. The Eighty-eighth was faced by the First German Parachute Corps, who defended the town of Bassano. It was a key position, for it was the gateway to a feared inner-mountain fortress system in which Hitler and his most zealous followers were expected to hold out.

The GI's had heard tales of this Alpine fortress, which was called the Inner Redoubt or the National Redoubt. They knew too well, from their own bitter experiences in struggling up and down the Appenine range to the south, what a formidable task might be up ahead in the north. Gratefully and with curiosity the motorized infantry began a march through the beaten enemy and met their Seventh Army colleagues at the Brenner Pass about an hour before noon on May 4, 1945. With this junction, the European and Mediterranean fronts became one line.

Viewing the defeated Germans, however, proved just as paradoxical as other events. For several days after the German surrender, it was hard to tell the vanquished from the victors. The Eighty-eighth Infantry Division found themselves far outnumbered by the Germans. Furthermore, a surprising number of the ex-soldiers of the Reich roamed the countryside at will, as arrogant in defeat as they had once been in victory. The Eighty-eighth advanced north and found itself near the town of Bolzano, which had been the headquarters for both German army units as well as the infamous *Schutzstaffel* (SS). The town was located in territory that had once belonged to Austria, but had been given to Italy after the First World War. The sympathy of the natives tended to veer toward the beaten Germans. Certainly, in contrast to the reception given the Americans in Bavaria and Austria, no welcomes were extended to the GI veterans of the Italian campaign.

German SS troops retained their arms and enjoyed

life in Bolzano with their girl friends, riding in their army vehicles where they wished, drinking in cafés and marching through the streets singing "Hitler Is My Fuehrer" and other Nazi songs. Some unit commanders of the defeated forces cheerfully volunteered their services and their men's for duty with the Allies against the Japanese. The SS maintained roadblocks and their military police stayed on duty. One German colonel even staged an award ceremony with his regiment drawn up in full order. At the Alpine town of Colle Isarco the departing Germans left in a cellar a time bomb that exploded, wounding twenty-two Americans and burning down a battalion command post. Officers and men of the Eighty-eighth swore and wondered who had won the war and why there were orders from outside the division to treat the SS gently.

On May 9, 1945, the lenient policy was revoked and the GI's exacted their revenge as they grimly carried out orders to curb the Germans. The SS was rounded up, ex-soldiers with false discharge papers or in civilian clothes were arrested, and massive man hunts were launched for suspected war criminals. With the new tough policy, a remarkable change came over the civilians around the Bolzano area. Suddenly they were amenable and the local girls easily switched affections with the change in uniforms. Peace and Allied military occupation had come to the Alpine region.

Perplexing questions, however, remained unanswered. Had there actually been an official policy of treating the SS with special consideration? Why had

8

the SS commander, Karl Wolff, been allowed to keep his luxurious headquarters and why had his troops been able to refuse quartering the Americans by citing terms of the German surrender in Italy? Exactly why had the tough German field units in Italy surrendered five days before their countrymen elsewhere had done so? And finally, what had happened to the feared Inner Redoubt defense system of which Wolff's SS was supposedly an integral part? What role had the Alpine fortress played in this drama, if any?

Curious tales and interesting evaluations of the fabled Redoubt were circulated and studied for a while. Then it did not seem to make much difference. The war in Europe was over and either home or the Pacific awaited the troops. The National Redoubt and its attendant problems receded in the minds of men and became a part of half-forgotten history.[4]

2

The National Redoubt, naturally enough, began in an Alpine atmosphere. Curiously though, it was the neutral nation of Switzerland which played an important part in the Redoubt's birth and evolution. In the late summer of 1940, after defeating France, the Germans considered the possibility of invading Switzerland. The Swiss were extremely uneasy over finding themselves surrounded by the victorious European Axis powers, and within government circles a fierce debate took place about the proper national policy for the neutral country to follow. The views of General Henri Guisan, Commanding General of the army, prevailed, after a bitter argument.

Guisan advocated the construction of an internal massive fortification system. The gigantic project was

10

put under way in 1940, and took two years to construct. When completed, the fortress complex included three major forts: Sargans in the east, Gotthard to the south, and St. Maurice in the west. The Swiss referred to their defense system as a *national reduit* and felt that its value lay in its deterrent power, since, if the nation were attacked, the inner region of the country could exist while the redoubt inflicted prohibitive casualties on the Axis armies.[1]

By 1943, the Western Allies, with the commencement of the painful Italian campaign, were once again on European soil. Already in London and elsewhere, Allied leaders were laying out various campaign plans for the final subjugation of Germany. The Germans, for their part, were naturally projecting future combat operations. Apparently, a final German stand in Southern Germany and the Alps was considered a distinct possibility.

In September, 1943, the German army began to explore the general idea of using defensive Alpine fortifications, beginning at Bregenz on the Liechtenstein border and extending eastward toward Klagenfurt, following the Italian-Yugoslav frontier, then swinging northward along the Hungarian border. The southern section of the projected fortification line in the Dolomite and Carnic Alps would make use of the old Austrian mountain positions built between 1915 and 1918 for use in World War I. It was also planned eventually to refurbish and incorporate the permanent Italian

11

fortifications into the new German system. The southern positions were in a relatively good state, however, and could prove useful.[2]

The anguished struggle in Italy caused concern in the U.S. War Department and German mountain-fighting techniques were assiduously studied in late 1943 and early 1944. Beginning in February, 1944, German army manuals on mountain warfare were translated into English and issued by Washington as regular field manuals. If fighting in the Appenines was bad, what could the Allies expect as they fought their way into the Alps?[3]

The year 1944 was a decisive one for the Western Allies as well as for the Germans. The primary stalemate on the Italian peninsula was broken in the spring; and during the summer the invasion of the continent was successfully accomplished, although opportunities were missed and much extremely hard combat lay ahead. D-Day and the successful Normandy campaign caused many German officials and military men to consider the future bleakly or grandiosely according to their nature. One of the latter was Reich Marshal Hermann Goering, who while visiting Italy told Field Marshal Albert Kesselring that, if the military fronts collapsed, Kesselring should organize an Alpine defense system and that he, Goering, for one, would die a proper Nazi death in the Alps.[4]

The Alpine regions held a special mystique for the National Socialists. On July 24 and 25, 1944, the German High Command (*Oberkommando der Wehr-*

macht or OKW) received a proposition from the Army High Command (*Oberkommande des Heeres* or OKH) that a survey team examine the southern positions in the Alps. There was no apparent connection between Goering's remark to Kesselring and this proposal. Goering's suggestion fitted the psychology of a certain type of Party member, while the recommendation for the survey was a purely military matter. There is reason to believe, however, that Propaganda Minister Paul Josef Goebbels heard details of the Army proposal and forbade any mention of Alpine defensive positions in the German press, since the word "defensive" was regarded as being defeatist.[5]

By September, 1944, it seemed that the Americans and British were in high gear, driving on to the German frontier. They were, however, unprepared for the rapidity of their own rapid advance and they outran their supplies. Field Marshal Gerd von Rundstedt collected the battered German armies and they feverishly began to renovate the Siegfried Line so vital to the defense of the Rhine. The Western advance slowed down to a bitterly contested walk. Far to the south in Italy, the advancing Allied forces paused at Kesselring's Gothic Line and penetrated it at many points, but exhaustion, casualties, and lack of ammunition brought the campaign to a halt in the mountains. The Germans held on stubbornly, and in the north, work was in progress to improve Southern Alpine and Northern Italian positions for use by the Fascist Italo-German army.[6]

13

Also, in September, even farther to the north, the OKW ordered the physical survey of both the Western Alpine position and more of the southern strong points to be linked eventually with those already being prepared. An engineering staff was established at Innsbruck, Austria, under the command of a Brigadier General, Marcinkiewicz. His job was to examine proposed sectors for defense and submit a list of them for approval. When permission had been obtained for the positions as surveyed, they were to be resurveyed in greater detail and then the sectors were to be staked out as they would be when occupied by troops. The exploration was for the purpose of mapping so that when the combatants arrived, they would know their precise location. No instructions were issued at this time for construction or improvement of the positions.[7]

Marcinkiewicz's task was difficult, even though he was assigned men who were expert Alpinists and wise to the ways of the mountains in winter. The weather, as expected, was a hazard, but there was inadequate equipment as well. The work dragged on during the remainder of the year, but it was finally halted by avalanches, snowstorms, drifting snow and the thick Alpine fogs. Not until late winter or spring would the final reconnoitering take place, and the sectors be ready for construction and ultimate occupation.[8]

Meanwhile, again in September, two seemingly unrelated events took place. On September 22, the Office of Strategic Services (OSS) in Washington issued a

14

long, scholarly report on South Germany. The report evaluated the area as a separate political, social, economic, and cultural entity within the Third Reich. The analysis mentioned that owing to Allied bombing various government agencies were known to have been relocated in the south and prophesied that as the Western Allied armies neared the German borders, these governmental evacuations could be expected to continue.

It is impossible to assess how widely this report was distributed among qualified military and diplomatic personnel at the time, since it was classified "Top Secret." But the report apparently was read by key top-level personnel, and its issuance coincided with a growing concern on the part of some Americans in Washington and in the European theater of operations about a final German defense effort in the south. One group of Americans was in Zurich, Switzerland, and whether they had read the OSS report is not known. From their neutral vantage point, however, they looked into Germany and thought they saw the phantom of a mighty Alpine defense system taking shape. They, too, issued a report in September.[9]

To obtain information from Switzerland, the German SS maintained a branch office of its *Sicherheitsdienst* (Security Service, or SD) as a courier center in the Bavarian town of Bregenz on the frontier. The office was only a relay station and the duties of its personnel were to receive incoming documents and dispatches and pass them on to the Reich Security

Main Office, or RSHA, in Berlin. The Bregenz center was commanded during that period by an SS Major named Gontard.

Gontard's predecessors had run afoul of the Nazi political and administrative leader for the *gau* of Tyrol-Vorarlberg, *Gauleiter* Franz Hofer. Gontard, however, got along with Hofer very well, and against regulations often allowed him to examine the incoming dispatches from Switzerland. Gontard, in Hofer's opinion, wished to curry favor in order to have the *Gauleiter* remove his prohibition against local Party members and political functionaries becoming associated with the SD in any capacity. Whatever the reasons, Gontard took an intercepted American diplomatic report to Hofer in September, 1944. The document was written by one of the Americans then in Zurich, who was extremely concerned about the specter of a Nazi Alpine fortress.[10]

For the Americans in Switzerland one fact was inescapable: some type of military activity was being undertaken by the Germans in certain areas of the Alps, especially in the south, where Austrian and Italian defensive positions were known to exist. More nebulous in nature, but important nonetheless, was the partially known psychology of certain of the Nazi leaders, especially that of Adolf Hitler.

Hitler was in the process of decimating the professional officer corps after various of its members were implicated in the July-twentieth plot against his life. Though the Americans were not entirely aware of the

16

details of Hitler's revenge, it was increasingly obvious that as Germany's supreme war lord, he intended to demand greater control than ever over the armed forces and the execution of combat operations. His orders to stand and die—even if militarily useless, as in the case of Stalingrad, North Africa, and Normandy —showed that he was capable of ordering a last-ditch fight in the Alpine area. There was nothing about the wartime performance of his *Waffen* SS (field or armed SS) that might lead Allied observers to believe that his orders would not be carried out with efficiency and fanaticism.

Bavaria was the birthplace of the Nazi Party and its leaders from Hitler on down often displayed mystical adoration for South Germany, its mountainous regions, and the adjacent Alpine sectors of Austria. Indeed, the SS leadership school was located at Bad Toelz in the Bavarian Alps. The "Eagle's Nest" at Berchtesgaden, Hitler's private retreat, symbolized to Germany's enemies no less than to the National Socialists, the psychological locus of the Nazis.[11]

There were other more concrete considerations which seem to have influenced American diplomatic personnel in Switzerland. Field Marshal Albert Kesselring's skill as a mountain fighter against the Allies was well demonstrated by his conduct of the Italian campaign. American diplomats, like their military colleagues in Washington earlier in the year, watched apprehensively as the Italian fighting inched its way north toward the Alps. Finally, there was the experi-

17

ence of the Swiss themselves in building their mountain fortifications and Americans in Switzerland were in close contact with that nation's military officers. It is interesting to note that the American report used the Swiss term *national reduit* when referring to the alleged Nazi fortifications. If the Swiss had been able to build up an Alpine stronghold of their own, it seemed logical that the desperate Nazis might well emulate them.[12]

The report itself, which was on its way to the United States Department of State, estimated that all of Germany's military fronts would collapse by mid-1945.[*] If the Germans managed to fortify the northern sections of the Alps, in addition to the already existing southern positions, fighting might be prolonged for at least half a year longer. It was determined that such a campaign would result in more casualties than all of the western fighting to date. There was a supposition that no American military commander would wish to take the responsibility for such a bloody battle. Instead, it was predicted by the Americans that the Allies could, perhaps, only lay siege to the *Alpen-Reduit*.[13]

One part of the State Department analysis bore a resemblance to the aforementioned OSS document. Both laid stress on the role of the Roman Catholic Church in Southern Germany. The message to the

[*] The only copy of the report comes from Hofer's interrogation file, which is now in the Office, Chief of Military History, Department of the Army files in Washington, D.C. The State Department refers inquiries on the report to the United States Department of the Army.

18

State Department, however, emphasized that if the Nazis could reach an especial accommodation with the local Catholic population, it might facilitate their defense of the fortress. Also envisioned were the possibilities of large caches of food and various military supplies and the creation of underground factories. In truth, and aside from either one of the reports, there were already stories afoot about the building of such factories, and a very few of them and some depots were actually to be constructed; but in the fall of 1944 they were not connected with any Nazi plan for an *Alpen-Reduit*.[14]

Other possibilities attendant on the building of the fortress system were enumerated in the intercepted message: it was thought that the Nazis might move their most important Allied prisoners to the redoubt and use them as hostages; continued Alpine resistance would serve as a beacon to the occupied zones of Germany, and might inspire further guerrilla activities. Also, during the prolonged hostilities tensions could arise between the Allies and the West and East and this unfortunate turn of events might cause serious trouble that could only aid the die-hard Nazi supporters. If the Germans could keep out refugees and useless governmental personnel, and if enough food were stored away, and if all the other suppositions set forth in the evaluation became realities, the *Alpen-Reduit* conceivably might hold out for almost two years.[15]

Gauleiter Hofer was very much impressed with the American idea of an inner-fortress system, and wished to bring it to the attention of Hitler himself. He delayed action on the report, however. First, he assumed that his friend Gontard had forwarded the intercepted document as a matter of routine. Then, too, he did not wish to have the RSHA know that Gontard was responsible for allowing him to see a copy of the transcript. His stated solicitude for Gontard may have been an act of kindness, but in fact he, no less than his SS comrade, could be compromised by a too precipitous maneuver involving espionage of the most allegedly secret nature. Almost two months went by with no action taken on the report and then, in November, Hofer submitted to the ominous Reich Leader, Martin Bormann, at Hitler's headquarters a copy of the American document with an accompanying letter. Hofer urged Bormann to present both papers to Hitler for an immediate decision.[16]

Hofer's excitement had grown as Gontard passed on more reports from Switzerland which indicated that the Americans were increasingly worried about an *Alpen-Reduit*. Hofer thought this unease should be exploited, for, as he pointed out, Germany could no longer hope for a favorable military decision, and it appeared (thanks to the ineptness of Goebbels' propaganda) that the Western Allies would not negotiate at Russia's expense. He urged Hitler to order the immediate construction of an *Alpenfestung* (Alpine Fortress).

Assume that the American reports prove correct in 1945, he wrote; if so, the building of an *Alpenfestung* would be a military necessity and could create a diplomatic opportunity. Hofer's remarks in regard to the diplomatic opportunity were extremely vague, but they implied that, by resisting, the Germans might drive a wedge between the Allies and attempt to negotiate separately to the advantage of those holed up within the *Alpenfestung*. If, on the other hand, the American evaluations of the military situation were incorrect, a mountain fortress with protected supplies and underground manufacturing centers might, in Hofer's inexpert eyes, still have a favorable effect on the course of military events. Precisely what the favorable effect could be, he did not elaborate. Time was the critical factor, Hofer felt, and half-measures would not work, for in such a case the enemy would be neither wearied enough to negotiate nor deterred in any military sense. He then proposed adoption of almost the exact steps outlined in the original American report.[17]

The balance of Hofer's suggestions was entirely his own. The *Alpenfestung* area was to be declared "off-limits"; troops from Italy were to withdraw there and work on the southern fortifications. He also recommended that the clumsy Foreign Minister, Joachim Ribbentrop, be removed as a necessary prerequisite to successful negotiations with the enemy. Also of special concern to Hofer was what he called "my territory," the Tyrol. Guerrilla activity was beginning in the south, and he was fearful that it might commence in his domain. If German troops were withdrawn from the south, the question of the Italian partisans would have to be handled by the Western Allies. Although he did not state it flatly, Hofer seems to have hinted that the partisans might be an embarrassment to the Western Allies, possibly because so many were Communists. Finally, the Germans should expedite the path to diplomatic negotiations by leaving all occupied pre-1918 Italian areas, falling back, and protecting only the "centuries-old Tyrolian territory which up to 1918 was a part of Austria." If the Fuehrer needed any further elucidation on the proposed *Alpenfestung*, Hofer was eager to appear personally and say his piece.[18]

Hofer, no less than the Americans in Switzerland, saw some details in connection with an Alpine fortress that did not exist in the fall of 1944. In his proposal to Hitler he talked of the southern defense line as being almost completed. Thus some 75,000 workers would soon be able to concentrate on the northern rim. In contrast to the completely unfortified northern area, some of the Austrian and Italian positions were in existence in the south, and also the German army was improving and building Alpine fortifications for the troops fighting in Italy. At the time Hofer wrote, however, little had been done to co-ordinate and refurbish these southern strongholds. According to Brigadier General Marcinkiewicz, who was on the spot surveying the various sectors, the reconnoitering was still incomplete, no orders had been issued for construction, and no labor was available for building. Hofer seems to have imagined a greater state of readiness than actually existed. The *Alpenfestung*, which was becoming a complete reality to the Americans and a hopeful one to Hofer, was beginning to weave its magic over certain of the belligerents on both sides.[19]

By late fall variations on the story of the Nazi citadel were spreading among the Allied and neutral press. The tales emanated primarily from Switzerland, but in early November, about the time that Hofer sent his proposal to Hitler through Bormann, the New York *Times* magazine section carried a short feature article from a correspondent in London entitled, "Hitler's Hideaway." The story was about Berchtesgaden, but it dwelt upon the extensive fortifications that had been built in the area near Hitler's dwelling.

According to the story, elaborate tunnels and extensive caves were filled with food and military supplies. As a final precaution, the author wrote, the entire district, 21 miles in length and 15 miles in depth, was mined and could be blown up by a button which was on the desk of the SS leader Heinrich Himmler in his underground office beneath Hitler's bungalow. Although the area was heavily guarded throughout the war, there was, in truth, no office under Hitler's bungalow for Himmler and no button for him to press. Such were the bizarre politics of Hitler's court that the nearest office which the *Reichsfuehrer* could actually secure in that Nazi preserve, dominated by his own SS, was in the suburbs of Salzburg, seventeen miles away! No matter, the increasingly lurid stories continued to circulate.[20]

23

Hofer's suggestions were virtually ignored at first at all of Germany's higher headquarters. It was his bad luck to have sent in his recommendations just as preparations for the surprising Ardennes Offensive were in full swing. At that moment no one close to Hitler at his headquarters or in the OKW was overly concerned about a defensive Alpine fortress in the event of invasion and occupation by the enemy. Hitler was convinced that the secret attack would be so disruptive that it would forestall any invasion of the Fatherland and give him a breathing spell.

Still, on the eve of the Battle of the Bulge, the Allied press carried a few stories of the secret Nazi fortress in the Alps. By then it was being called by the title given it in the original American report—the National Redoubt. The Communist Party of America also was indicating concern over the Redoubt, and in the *Daily Worker* of December 15, 1944, the paper's military expert predicted a German defense of the entire Alpine region. Especially emphasized was the Russian drive in Hungary which, in the *Daily Worker's* opinion, was proving to be the eastern assault on the Alpine citadel. The military analyst of the *Daily Worker* thus joined the growing number of those who believed in the Redoubt's existence.[21]

The Ardennes battle, which started on December 16, occupied the attention of everyone and the Redoubt was forgotten for the moment. The Nazi Propaganda Minister, Paul Josef Goebbels, however, managed to take note of it once again. During the fall Goebbels had noticed sporadic Allied press reports of the National Redoubt even after his prohibition of the subject in the German news media six months earlier. Hitler, in a recent speech, had announced a "no surrender" policy and Goebbels apparently decided to exploit Allied concern over the alleged Redoubt by connecting it with Hitler's declaration.

Goebbels, it seems, fed some tidbits of information about the mythical fortress system to the Allied and neutral press. Watching the positive reaction, the Propaganda Minister was reported to have called a secret meeting in December of all the German editors and journalists. He told them that even if they had heard of the fabulous Redoubt through neutral press sources, they were forbidden ever to mention the subject in print. Reiterating his theme of the summer, Goebbels declared that talk of defensive positions might undermine belief in the ultimate victory and thus produce defeatism.[22]

The second time he dealt with the Redoubt, however, Goebbels had a card up his sleeve. Having sworn the German journalists to secrecy, he organized within his ministry a special section that produced a host of stories concerning the Alpine defense system. The special unit went into operation in January, 1945. The theme of the stories was always the same: impregnable positions, massive supplies carefully hidden in bombproof caves, underground factories, and, of course, elite units of troops to man the whole bastion.[23]

Precisely what was happening at Hitler's headquarters in December in regard to the *Alpenfestung* remains vague, one of the reasons being that there are so few records about the Redoubt and the part played in it by key Nazi leaders during that month. It appears that Hofer's memorandum was presented to Hitler who, transfixed by the vision of inevitable victory, was scornful of any talk that even hinted at military collapse and defeat. Hofer's scheme had been seconded by an Austrian *Gauleiter*, Friedrich Ranier, but probably not until Goebbels, or someone who retained Hitler's trust, suggested that the Alpine stronghold held a nuisance value did Hitler show any interest in it. Exactly when he did warm up to the whole idea is extremely difficult to pinpoint, but it was apparently sometime in the early part of the new year.[24]

What began to happen in January was rather typical of the Nazi government in the last year of the war. Acting independently of each other, agencies started to exploit what was fast becoming an *idee fixe* among the Americans as 1945 unfolded. First, Goebbels' special propaganda section went into action and then, operating on its own, the SD decided to join the move to confuse the Allies. While the propagandists released sinister stories of the fortress, the security service leaked phony blueprints and bogus intelligence data to American agents who seemed most ready to accept the stories about the Redoubt.[25]

When reports were brought to Hitler of the increased Allied fears, he ordered *Gauleiter* Hofer to take whatever actions he felt necessary to start construction on defensive Alpine works in his province. Hofer knew exactly what he wanted. He was con-

26

cerned about the American Sixth Army Group's campaign commanded by Lieutenant General Jacob L. Devers. Sixth Army Group had had difficulties at Strasbourg near the border in early January, but by the end of the month its First French Army under General Jean de Lattre de Tassigny, with the help of strong American reinforcements, began to pinch off the Colmar pocket. Eventually the German Nineteenth Army was refused permission by Hitler to withdraw and the Franco-American force was able to inflict crushing damage on it. The Allies stood ready to assault the Rhine from Switzerland to the North Sea. Hofer's immediate concern was the possibility that the French-based Sixth Army Group might attack the Tyrol through the southeastern corner of Switzerland.[26]

In January, 1945, Marcinkiewicz received orders to build up the defensive positions in the west between Bregenz and Feldkirch on the Swiss front. The instructions came through the National Defense Minister for the Tyrol-Vorarlberg area, who was Franz Hofer. Actual construction got under way in mid-February with about 2,000 civilian workmen engaged from the paramilitary Todt labor organization. Not everyone was pleased by Hofer's actions or fully aware of his grand design. The Chief of Operations of the Armed Forces High Command, General Alfred Jodl, wrote to Himmler that he was opposed to any fortifying of the border between Switzerland and Germany. He never mentioned anything in the letter about an *Alpenfes-*

tung. In fact, Marcinkiewicz, who was to be in the supposed Redoubt area longer than anyone else, was never acquainted with the idea of a national mountain fortress and neither saw nor heard from a military superior the expression *Alpenfestung*. Apparently not even the directives that were passed on to Marcinkiewicz through Hofer's office used the term. The first and only time during the war that Marcinkiewicz heard the word *Alpenfestung* was from the lips of a Nazi district leader (*Kreisleiter*) in Kitzbuehel a month before Germany capitulated.

The general was not alone. A great number of officers within the German army either remained in ignorance of the National Redoubt or claimed that they ridiculed the idea as being militarily unsound at that stage of Germany's dissolution. Not even the official news commentator for the armed forces, Kurt Dittmar, was aware of the stronghold until near the end of January, when he first read about it in a Swiss newspaper.[27]

Journalists were having a field day aided, in good part, by the efforts of Goebbels and the SD. The New York *Daily Worker* stated that the Germans were mounting suicidal attacks for the relief of Budapest, which indicated how scared they were of the Russian eastern drive on their Alpine stronghold. Also, the Nazi moves on Strasbourg indicated a defense of the western half of the Redoubt. But the rest of the press and periodicals were no less impressed by the Alpine stronghold than the Communists.

28

As an example, *Collier's* magazine at the end of January ran an extremely detailed article on a gigantic guerrilla warfare program which, it alleged, was being set up at Bad Aussee about fifty or sixty miles from Berchtesgaden. There, according to the article, the cream of the SS and the Hitler Youth Organization were being trained for post-defeat guerrilla warfare. Their weapons were to be the most ingenious that German technicians could devise and their training was based upon the German experience in dealing with the partisan bands in their occupied countries. Eventually secret headquarters for the roving guerrilla armies would be located higher in the Alps than Bad Aussee, possibly even in a neutral country. The German guerrillas were called "Werewolves" and would burst forth upon the scene when the Allies were concentrating on occupation duties. They would be headed by the apelike Austrian, Ernst Kaltenbrunner, head of the RSHA. The author of the article correctly predicted a collapse of the movement because the German people would not support it.[28]

Farfetched as the tale was in most respects, before the incredible last months of the Nazi rule ran their course some of the more fantastic incidents of the story actually took place, though not exactly as outlined in *Collier's*.

Kaltenbrunner appears in the myth of the Redoubt, but hardly as an efficient, valiant leader of irregulars. The Werewolves were a product of Himmler's limited and murky mind. Created in November, 1944, their existence did not terrify the Allies quite as much as it did cynically realistic Germans, who preferred co-operating with the British and Americans rather than sabotaging them. They were, furthermore, not to be guerrilla forces in the usual sense. Guerrilla warfare implied defeat, the idea of which was an anathema to Hitler. So, the Werewolves were actually intended to operate behind Allied lines in uniform as soldiers while the German armies fought on. Neither the German public nor the Americans realized this, however. Goebbels' propaganda machinery, acting apart from the SS, used the idea to whip up nihilistic war spirit, but the propaganda caused untold misconceptions about the Werewolves' true purpose and role. Ultimately, the Werewolves no less than the National Redoubt, proved to be a delusion, but a delusion also believed in by SHAEF.[29]

Yet the stories continued as the disjointed efforts of the SD and Goebbels took effect. Rumors at SHAEF seemed to confirm the build-up of large-scale guerrilla training activities in Southern Germany. G-2, meanwhile, was continuing to sift through information from prisoners of war and from neutral as well as German civilian sources that indicated men were being transferred to the Redoubt area. Not all SHAEF G-2 personnel believed the stories, but those who did urged that the possibility of a Redoubt be considered seriously. G-2 heard that field fortifications were being constructed at Bregenz—but this was exactly as the SD had planned. When SS geologists and students from the SS mountain school showed up to survey and blast for new construction, the German secret service made sure that the activities were leaked to the Americans. But then another strange complication entered the story of the Redoubt and further confused the increasingly distorted picture.[30]

3

In Italy, SS First Lieutenant Guido Zimmer despondently thought of his future during the month of January. He was sick of the war. Zimmer was attached to the headquarters of SS General and General of the Field SS Karl Wolff, formerly Himmler's liaison officer with Hitler. In 1945, Wolff was the Military Governor of Northern Italy at Bolzano. Zimmer, so the story goes, overheard of a plan attributed to *Gauleiter* Franz Hofer while the latter was visiting Wolff. Hofer wanted the Germans to scorch the earth of Northern Italy as they retreated and then withdraw behind the impregnable defenses of Hofer's cherished *Alpenfestung*. Such an action promised to prolong the war indefinitely and this did not sit well with the discouraged Zimmer.

Apparently, the low-ranking Lieutenant was not alone in his feelings. SS Colonel Eugen Dollmann,

Wolff's liaison officer with Field Marshal Kesselring, also was disenchanted with the course of the war and Germany's obviously waning fortunes. He once expressed the hope that the war might be ended—at least in Italy—if there were some way to get in touch with the Western Allies. Zimmer reportedly knew of Dollmann's sentiments. Both of them knew influential Italians who could reach the Americans or British, and Zimmer finally approached one of them.[1]

The man Zimmer contacted was an Italian baron and industrialist named Luigi Parrilli, who played the difficult but intriguing role of a friend of the belligerents on both sides while maintaining friendship with the neutral Swiss. Parrilli told Zimmer he would see to it that the views held by the two SS officers reached the Allies. As events showed, Parrilli did not deal directly with them, but he did relate the information to a Swiss named Max Husmann, who had valuable friends in the Swiss army and the government. Husmann passed the remarks of the Germans on to Dr. Max Waibel, a major in the Swiss army's intelligence section. The tidings brought to Waibel inevitably found their way to two other persons—General Henri Guisan, head of the Swiss army and creator of its *national reduit*, and Allen Dulles, then established in Berne by the OSS.[2]

After much evaluation on the American side and much back-stage whispering among the Germans at Wolff's headquarters, negotiations began between Wolff's emissaries and Dulles in Switzerland. Waibel was the Swiss representative during the talks that stretched out through the late winter and early spring of 1945. He was affronted by bloodshed and the wanton destruction that threatened Northern Italy if the fighting continued. Guisan was intensely interested in what the Germans in Italy might be up to for somewhat less humanitarian reasons than affected Major Waibel.[3]

The German plans were confused. One of the ideas seemed to be that of securing peace with the Allies in Italy and then shifting the German troops from there to the Eastern front against the Russians. Dulles, naturally, held out for a complete military surrender. *Gauleiter* Hofer's ideal was a general retreat and an intensive fight in the *Alpenfestung* against everyone. He was definitely not in favor of any surrender negotiations, which he considered treasonous. He was therefore kept in the dark about Wolff's machinations for as long as possible. Hofer, in a mixed-up fashion, hoped that somehow the Germans from Italy would repair to the *Alpenfestung*, or the whole Alpine area, and wait there for months. In that interval the Allies might have a falling-out and could then treat with the Nazi survivors in the fortress.[4]

General Guisan's responsibilities and his suspicions of the Germans led him to make a rather different evaluation of the situation than anyone else. He wanted a German surrender in Italy for reasons entirely beneficial to Switzerland. Since 1943, he had been convinced that if the Nazis were driven out of Italy, they would try to seize the Alpine routes leading into Switzerland. This would enable the Germans to utilize parts of the Swiss *national reduit* for a last-ditch fight, or to force their way into the neutral nation and turn it into a giant internment camp for the army. In either case, Guisan knew that Switzerland's neutrality would be compromised and that an actual bloody fight might ensue. Also he was increasingly skeptical of stories about the fabled *Alpenfestung*.[5]

It had taken the Swiss over two years to build theirs and Guisan knew the Germans were barely beginning. Furthermore, the Nazis were attempting the job without proper material or manpower. Guisan also felt that the Bavarian Alps would not prove to be as effective an area for fortifications as the Swiss Alps. The German topography revealed too-wide valleys and the mountains did not, in Guisan's estimation, offer the same degree of protection from air attack as did those in Switzerland. A redoubt could not be improvised. If the Nazis were not bluffing about their fortress, they would have to capture the Swiss system to make their own truly effective. Whatever the German reasons and capabilities were, Guisan wanted the Germans to surrender in Italy and stay away from his country. Thus, Waibel's altruistic presence in the plot had Guisan's hardheaded, pragmatic backing. The negotiations proceeded as the winter progressed.[6]

By February, 1945, the myth of the National Redoubt was gaining momentum. Fact and fancy mingled to lend credence to many evaluations of the Alpine stronghold. A spokesman for Ribbentrop predicted a savage guerrilla fight as the Allies got closer, and during the middle of the month there was relatively large-scale evacuation of government ministries from Berlin as personnel with records and files fled south. Goebbels watched the dispersal with open contempt. He had already debated in his mind the alternatives to flight and decided to stay in Berlin and die even if it meant poisoning his wife and children. His state of mind was best illustrated by his proposal that Germany repudiate the Geneva convention and massacre captured Allied airmen as a reprisal for the destruction of Dresden.[7]

Hitler's intentions were not known, but he ordered that no prisoners then in concentration camps located in the path of the advancing Allies were to be liberated. An utterly chaotic transfer of the inmates primarily from Buchenwald and Dachau to the uncompleted *Alpenfestung* was initiated. Eventually, this movement was stopped by Himmler and others within the SS, for the *Reichsfuehrer* SS was to try to bargain secretly, if blunderingly, with the Allies for a peace settlement. His plans, however, were not to be connected with Wolff's proposed Italian surrender negotiations. Also, by mid-February, actual construction had begun on the western defense line of the *Alpenfestung* between Bregenz and Feldkirch. By the end of February the positions on the southern rim of the Alps prepared for the German army in Italy were almost completed. Allied intelligence and the neutral press noted most of these events—especially the evacuations from Berlin, the propaganda blasts about German partisan warfare, and the military activity in the Alps.[8]

The known facts began to support the speculations which ranged from the realistic to the ridiculous. The esteemed military analyst for the New York *Times*, Hanson Baldwin, ventured the sober forecast that after Berlin's inevitable fall, the fighting would shift to the Alpine area.[9] The Associated Press in Moscow quoted Russian officials who warned the West that the Germans were preparing an Alpine defense. The center of German authority seemed to be shifting south, and a mysterious "Vatican source" was quoted as stating that Hitler had sought refuge in a monastery in Salzburg.*

Himmler, who like Hofer and a few other Party men did believe in the *Alpenfestung*, was usually the "mastermind" in the press accounts of the Nazi citadel. Excellent guesses were made about the size and the territories included in the Redoubt, but no one really knew what was actually taking place. Himmler never seems to have doubted the *Alpenfestung*, but he was not its creator nor did he truly know anything about it in a practical sense. His view of the fortress was myopic and mystical. The top command of the SS was riven by intrigue, plots, and counterplots. But in such

* This last fantasia had Hitler still suffering from head wounds incurred in the July 20, 1944, plot. Several priests were reported as seeing him in Salzburg after the monastery's monks were turned out to make room for the German leader.

a mad world anything seemed possible, and as it turned out, Ernst Kaltenbrunner foolishly tried to use the stronghold for his own peculiar ends.

The newspaper accounts, however, knowingly detailed Himmler's and the SS's role in the Redoubt. The whole enterprise seemed fiendishly well organized and typical of Himmler's demonic skill. He was certainly demonic and he was capable of envisioning a Nazi mountain defense. His military talents, however, were nonexistent as his command of the Rhine and Vistula Army Groups illustrated, and he was plainly incapable of organizing anything militarily efficient in the way of an Alpine defense system. Nevertheless, the rumors abounded as the winter ended and the last weary spring of the European war began.[10]

In early March, Hitler's staff in Berlin planned to move the Reich's Chancellory to Thuringia. Goebbels protested; he felt that any such move was nonsensical. He knew that the end was not far off and was planning a Nazi-style *Götterdämmerung* among the ruins of Berlin. Certainly Germany's end seemed imminent to those who were forced to face reality on March 7. On that day the Americans with great luck and skill crossed the Rhine on the damaged Ludendorff Bridge at Remagen. Establishment of the Remagen bridgehead offered a host of opportunities to the Supreme Allied Commander.[11]

Increasingly, the National Redoubt was preying on the minds of all the Allies. Again, just after the Americans crossed the Rhine, Moscow warned several times of a military build-up in South Germany and preparation for a last-ditch stronghold. In the latest covey of rumors the Salzburg salt mines were being prepared for defense. The *Daily Worker* periodically and dutifully echoed the Kremlin's words and its military editor noted that the fierce fighting south of Lake Balaton in Hungary betrayed Nazi intentions to retreat into the Alps. Even Winston Churchill felt that the determined German operations in Italy and in Hungary which guarded the approaches to Vienna made no sense unless the defense of South Germany figured in their plans. But with Hitler one never knew. The Russians may have had good reason from their viewpoint to wonder about the Redoubt at this time. The Germans did have a large army in Italy and they were putting up an extremely hard fight in Hungary. Also, the Russians apparently were hearing peculiar tales about the German army in Italy treating separately with the Western Allies in violation of wartime agreements.[12]

Indeed, Karl Wolff actually met directly with Allen Dulles in Zurich on March 8; and they discussed the surrender of the German army in Italy. Precisely what the Russians knew about the Dulles-Wolff talks is unclear. They may have intercepted some messages or had reported to them stories about shifting fronts. Perhaps the naturally suspicious mind of Stalin simply came to the conclusion that a secret deal was being made at Russian expense.

Dulles felt that the operation was too important for his agency to handle alone and requested support from Field Marshal Sir Harold Alexander, the Allied Supreme Commander in Italy. Alexander complied and the talks between Wolff, the OSS, and the Allied representative sent by Alexander to Switzerland dragged on and off for weeks. A Russian demand for representation was refused by the Western Allies, and on March 16 they demanded that the talks be stopped. The Americans and the British tried to reassure the Kremlin that nothing was being concluded that would aid the German war effort against the Soviets. The talks were exploratory, and if a military capitulation took place, Soviet representatives would be invited to attend. But Stalin remained unconvinced and never rescinded his allegations of Allied bad faith.[13]

Despite mistrustful outbursts from Moscow, the Western Allies were angry but patient. Whatever plans Wolff may have had—if any—about shifting fronts apparently were never presented, since neither Dulles nor Alexander's agents would consider such a move. Wolff stated that if the Allies stopped bombing civilian targets in Northern Italy, the Germans would put up only token resistance in the Po valley. The National Redoubt was not to be defended, since most of the forces needed by it would surrender on the Italian plain. If this plan were executed, it would make any consideration of an *Alpenfestung* by the Nazis or OKW purely theoretical. The fortress would be militarily valueless without southern defensive positions manned by the troops then in Italy.

Wolff, having presented his case, had to scurry around trying to secure Kesselring's support while continuing to hide his intentions from Himmler. At this time Kesselring, who was ambivalent and felt obliged by his oath to Hitler not to surrender, was appointed commander of all the German forces in the West and left Italy. His Italian command was to be filled by General Heinrich Gottfried von Vietinghoff, a much less belligerent personality than Kesselring. But he, too, had to be persuaded. The Allied representatives impatiently sat in Switzerland awaiting German emissaries with the latest proposals. They did not, however, reappear for a long time.[14]

Some news of Wolff's double-dealing leaked out and found its way to Himmler. He summoned Wolff home and the latter tearfully protested any intent of treason and pretended that his sole purpose had been to drive a wedge between the Russians and the Allies. Wolff's trickery, however, was being severely compromised by an arch rival within the SS, Ernst Kaltenbrunner, the head of the RSHA. There is reason to believe that it was Kaltenbrunner who tipped Himmler off to Wolff's dealings with the British and Americans. In any case, Wolff was forbidden by Hitler's order to travel to Switzerland any more—a prohibition he ignored.[15]

At the end of March, Himmler made Kaltenbrunner chief of security operations for all of the southern part of the Third Reich. Among Kaltenbrunner's tasks was the preparation of the *Alpenfestung* in which Himmler believed. But Kaltenbrunner was as untrustworthy an opportunist as ever reached eminence in the sanguinary world of the SS. He had his own plans for the stronghold and felt he was in a position to promulgate them.

Kaltenbrunner's scheme could make sense only to inhabitants of his grotesque world: to exploit Allied and Swiss fears about a fight in the Redoubt, but at the same time to try to preserve his native Austria from Russian occupation by seeking common cause with the Allies against the Soviets. While Allied military planners might have guessed at what was going on inside Germany, they generally remained in ignorance of these diverse and confused plans being pursued independently by the various Nazi factions. As March progressed and the early spring lengthened into April, new estimates and predictions of enemy intent and capabilities were formulated by the Western Allies.[16]

The Beginning

of the End

Part 2

4

The seizure of the bridge at Remagen on March 7, by the American Ninth Armored Division, changed the entire outlook of the Allied offensive in the west. Bradley brilliantly spotted the significance of the bridgehead, though not all parties at SHAEF did. On March 11, however, SHAEF Intelligence figured that the main German defensive effort now seemed directed at protecting the Alpine zone. What else would explain the heavy resistance in Italy or the dispatch of the Sixth SS Panzer to the Danube valley? Also, various SS and specialized units were reported to have appeared in the Alpine area, and leading Nazi personalities were now known to be fleeing into the Redoubt. New decisions were in the offing and although they had not yet been announced, the March 11 Intelligence Summary may have been a harbinger of change in Allied planning.[1]

Originally, Eisenhower (it appeared) was going to force the Rhine in his main attack north of the Ruhr and drive across the northern plains of Germany with Berlin as the goal. Using the Rhine as a covering front, he could build up additional forces which, in turn, he could send across the Rhine south of the Ruhr as a secondary attack. The latter offensive would give his maneuver greater flexibility, since the German forces would be thinned out trying to cope with both drives. Having the two thrusts—north and south—would allow Eisenhower to shift the weight of his attack northeastward toward Berlin or eastward toward Leipzig. The British had disputed Eisenhower's plans in January and recommended that the main emphasis be on a northern push. By February the Supreme Commander met British objections by agreeing to use maximum strength in the north; but he left the way open for increased operations in the south if warranted.[2] This was, in blunt fact, to cause trouble between the British and the Americans.*

* The differences were partially ironed out at meetings held before the February Yalta Conference. Marshall met Eisenhower at Marseille near the very end of January and the entire Combined Chiefs of Staff met at Malta, where General Smith and Major General Harold Bull, G-3 of SHAEF, represented the Supreme Commander and presented his case. The Malta meeting also signified the end of any intensified military operations emanating from Italy into the Balkan area. The Americans did not wish to get mixed up in a Balkan political situation, while the British, led by Churchill, adopted the opposite viewpoint. The United States' General Mark Clark, Commanding General of the Fifteenth Army Group in Italy, appears to have been the sole American who

Between March 7 and March 28 much happened both at SHAEF and in the field. The Germans savagely counterattacked the Remagen bridgehead, but by March 21, it was too well established for them to be able to destroy it. Farther to the south, Sixth Army Group successfully inflicted a crushing defeat on the German First and Seventh armies. The whole Rhineland campaign was a crashing disaster for the Nazis. Almost a quarter of a million prisoners were taken and the German army in the west was largely destroyed. In the east, by March 11, Marshal Zhukov's advance Russian forces were twenty-eight miles from Berlin. It seemed the city would fall despite frantic defensive preparations. As a result of these victorious events, some fast reshuffling of operations took place at SHAEF.

A host of evaluations, decisions, and changes occupied Eisenhower's immediate attention and several of them blew up winds of controversy which have not yet died down. The most disputed and salient event was the Supreme Commander's shift in the balance of his attack from the north to the south. This decision produced a brilliant campaign by Bradley's Twelfth Army Group in its advance through Germany. But the change of emphasis from Field Marshal Sir Bernard L. Montgomery's proposed major northern thrust to Bradley's campaign upset the British no end. Critics

---

wished to support the British view at the time. After the war, other American soldiers, such as Lt. General Lucien Truscott, Jr., revised their wartime judgments and swung to Clark's position.

have charged that, by swinging south, Eisenhower handed Berlin to the Soviets on a platter. Also, there has been the accusation that SHAEF became so pre-occupied by the ghost of the the National Redoubt that it not only unnecessarily abandoned Berlin to the Russians, but it also delivered Prague to them, thus allowing the Russians to pose in Eastern Europe as the major force in the Nazi defeat.[3]

Eisenhower shifted his forces for military, not political, reasons. One of the most important phases of his over-all plan was the encirclement of the industrial Ruhr and this remained one of his prime objectives. But having crossed the Rhine and witnessed the great destruction of the German army, he next considered how best to inflict final defeat. He saw nothing to dissuade him from abandoning his idea of enveloping the Ruhr, but new elements entered the picture which demanded appraisal. There was evidence that the Germans had been moving armament factories deeper into the Reich and that possibly a drive south and east to seal them off might be the more effective way of ensuring the German capitulation. Enemy resistance was proving stiffer than it should have been in view of the increasingly hopeless situation by the Germans.

Extensive explanations for the shift to the south were offered by Eisenhower, Bradley, and the Supreme Commander's Chief of Staff, Lieutenant General Walter Bedell Smith, following the war. They are well known but need to be summarized: Berlin may have held a political and psychological importance, but it was of no important military value; if the Western

Allies got to Berlin first, they would have to vacate much territory which the Russians would occupy by prior political agreement. Since the Western Allies were about two hundred miles away from the German capital, while the Russians were in its outskirts, it appeared foolish to try for Berlin. Furthermore, the terrain between the British and Americans and Berlin was ill suited for armored operations. The Elbe River promised to be a formidable obstacle: to bridge it and sustain an advance beyond the waterway, logistical support would have to be withdrawn from all other units along the rest of the front, thus immobilizing them. And, finally, many persons at SHAEF believed that the Soviets undoubtedly would get to Berlin first and if the Western Allies tried to take it, their casualties might be very high—possibly 100,000.[4]

There were, in addition to the Ruhr envelopment, other prime reasons for moving fast. Bradley's spearheads had to move rapidly eastward toward the Leipzig-Dresden area to effect a junction with the Red Army in order to cut Germany in half and prevent its military units from coalescing. Such an action had been predetermined in September, 1944, if it appeared that the Soviets would reach Berlin ahead of the Western Allies. Also, it was believed necessary for Montgomery to seize the northern coastal town of Lübeck to cut off those German units in Denmark and Norway and obtain the valuable ports of Bremen and Hamburg.

Finally, there was the necessity for sealing off the National Redoubt to prevent any build-up of forces there that might prolong the war. In relation to the other objectives, Eisenhower rated this last one as "equally important." Smith stated that "above all else" the Redoubt had to be isolated. After all, there was still the Pacific war raging and MacArthur would need reinforcements from the European Theater to augment his own forces for the proposed dreaded invasion of Japan. These, then, were the reasons considered important enough to warrant a modification within Eisenhower's over-all plan.[5]

The new strategy, developed between March 21 and the first week in April, had some aspects which caused trouble. These were: the question of British versus American prestige; the manner in which the operational change was announced by the Supreme Commander; the differing teleological views on war of the Americans and the British; and the actual military significance of the National Redoubt as an objective important enough to influence tactical and strategic thinking.

On March 21, Bradley's Twelfth Army Group issued an order entitled "Reorientation of Strategy." The directive is pertinent because it especially drew attention to the role the Redoubt played in the strategic change. It contained the following headings: The Object of Allied Strategy, Manner of Execution, Outline Plan of Action, plus two appendixes—one of which was an intelligence evaluation of the National Redoubt and the second of which was a map illustrating the general lines of action to be taken in the campaign against the Redoubt.[6]

50

The reorientation carefully pointed out that the Supreme Commander had received no directives from the Combined Chiefs of Staff in regard to military or political objectives. Rather, they had instructed him to attack the "heart of Germany." What specifically constituted the heart was left for him to define. Acting upon the advice of his intelligence agencies, he had decided that the Ruhr was Germany's main life-giving organ, that is should be isolated, and that a drive on to Berlin should follow.

Since those early plans had been formulated, however, the directive continued, new discoveries had been made of the enemy's will to resist even after losing vital components of his war-making machine. The situation had altered enough to make the original plans obsolete, and it was felt that even with the loss of the Ruhr, the chances were that the enemy could and would continue to fight. Seizure of the Ruhr was no longer considered fatal to the enemy cause. Berlin, likewise, was no longer important as a means for continuing the German war effort. By contrast: "As reported by G-2 . . . all indications suggest that the enemy's political and military directorate is already in the process of displacing (*sic*) to the 'Redoubt' in lower Bavaria." Accordingly, it was felt that the Nazi plan was to withdraw stubbornly under the pressure exerted by all the Allies, gaining all possible time, in order to prepare "for development of the Redoubt."[7]

What SHAEF and Twelfth Army Group headquarters foresaw was a slow German retreat southward

51

ultimately ending in the Redoubt. To forestall execution of this maneuver, the enemy's main line of retreat had to be severed and his troops driven northward where they could be rounded up against the Baltic and North Seas shores. If this plan worked, resistance in Bavaria was expected to be weakened greatly. Since the German communications were to be severed, their strength and their mobility would, correspondingly, be seriously impaired. It was decided that ". . . success attends a bold advance by an army beyond the range of close support from adjacent elements." That being so, the same policy was suggested for army groups since bold strokes "offer large dividends at low risk." Large areas of territory were more desirable objectives than "localized centers of diminishing industrial or political significance." These observations could be taken as implied criticism of the British plan and Montgomery's predilection for the methodical, cautious "set-piece" type of attack. All of these considerations were taken into account, and the directive continued, "particularly the enemy's evident intention to withdraw into Bavaria" made a reorientation of strategy mandatory.[8]

G-2 offered its evaluation, which was appended to the order. Reading the intelligence report confirms the fact that Goebbels and the SD had done their work well. Even so, in fairness to the intelligence officers who drew up the appraisal, there is in it a note of hesitancy and professional skepticism. What the report contained was a rehash of the SHAEF Intelligence

Summary of March 11. Information about the Redoubt, the evaluation stated, had come from German prisoners of war and from agents. We know now that the prisoners of war and the agents were especially valuable transmitters of the type of information the Nazi security service wished to spread. There was the often-repeated possibility of guerrilla warfare directed from Berchtesgaden. The usual exaggerations in regard to fortifications, crack SS units, and the stockpiling of ammunition were dutifully recorded as well.[9]

There were, however, nuggets of speculative truth concerning the Redoubt. Truly, Himmler's absurd and misunderstood Werewolf plan did exist in some form, even if it was to come to nothing; many party officials such as Himmler, Hofer, and Kaltenbrunner did believe, each in his own fashion, that a fight in the Redoubt was feasible.

Twelfth Army's G-2 had also noted that German defensive tactics had changed. The enemy was giving first priority to the utilization of obstacles, followed by concealment, cover, communications, and finally, fields of fire. Intelligence officers suggested that these practices established a trend toward guerrilla warfare. They correctly surmised that many men would be attracted to the Alpine fortress. It was also true that many German leaders and their families, not to mention government ministries, had sought refuge in the Redoubt. The rumor that important hostages held by the Germans were to be transferred there not only had been part of the original American diplomatic report on the Redoubt, but with modifications had become a part of *Gauleiter* Hofer's plan proposed to Hitler. What was not true in the new Twelfth Army Group directive was the reference to the Redoubt as a "German stronghold." Its defensive preparations were nil in March and April. Even the G-2 appendix carefully steered away from such a description, and called its evidence inconclusive until the Redoubt's actual existence could be verified by aerial photographs and by agents within the area.[10]

Farther to the south, the Seventh Army intelligence report for March 25 went considerably beyond those of SHAEF and Twelfth Army. In fact, Seventh Army's appraisal can only be called a massive misreading of German capabilities based upon the wildest of rumors gleaned from only "fairly reliable sources." According to Seventh Army G-2, Himmler had ordered provisions for 100,000 men and the area was to be defended by "eighty crack units of from 1,000 to 4,000 men each." Himmler was seeing to it that the best arms Germany could produce were earmarked for the Redoubt and sealed trains bearing armaments were arriving from the Skoda works. "Many of those trains" were seen to be carrying a new type of gun. Elaborate underground ordnance shops run by hydroelectric power were being built and a report alleged that an aircraft factory capable of producing "a complete Messerschmitt" was in operation. The terrain would aid the defense and the Nazis could draw upon the productive capacities of the Po and Danube valleys,

Western Czechoslovakia, and the upper Balkans. The Redoubt Center's combat personnel would number between 200,000 and 300,000 veterans of the SS and special mountain troops "thoroughly imbued with the Nazi spirit," who could be expected to fight fanatically to the last man.[11]

A map with a defensive positions overprint was issued along with the study. It showed possible and probable defense lines, intermediate phase lines, final defense lines before the Redoubt which extended as far northwest as Stuttgart, and then the final Redoubt Center running from Feldkirch in the west to about Bad Aussee in the east. The report ended by stating that the Redoubt Center would most likely be defended because the Nazi leadership had the "will and the imperative need to continue to resist," that the German people and their army were "incapable of disobedience" and so would follow the Nazi orders, and that the disposition of the Allied forces was pressuring the enemy into the Redoubt area. Of all the information and assumptions in the Seventh Army evaluation only the very last comment was true.*[12]

At the same time that the various pessimistic American intelligence appreciations were being made about

* According to a former colleague, Major General Sir Kenneth Strong, the SHAEF G-2 was inclined not to agree entirely with the Seventh Army's intelligence conclusions. The informant, who must remain anonymous, does not know precisely with which or how many of the Seventh Army's conclusions Strong did not agree.

the Alpine fortress and the enemy's will and capability to resist, conditions on the German side were increasingly chaotic. Defeatism and opportunism continued to riddle the hierarchy of the supposedly fanatically loyal SS which, in the American view, was to be the main core of the Redoubt's furious defense system. The plots and counterplots inside the elite organization would have resembled a badly written spy thriller had not so much evil, perversion, and human suffering been involved.

Himmler, in American eyes the cold, calculating master of the whole Redoubt myth, was, at this time, a physical and nervous wreck, living in craven dread of Hitler. So bad was his condition by late March that he was unable to perform sustained work and retreated periodically to a hospital where he received treatment and attempted to escape reality. Continued intrigue swept the upper echelons of the SS and the Nazi Party as various individuals flirted with the dream of surrendering to the Western Allies and fighting with them against the Russians, or capitulating entirely before total destruction overwhelmed them all. And Himmler himself was not immune from entertaining such ideas.[13]

From about December, 1944, Himmler had been ineffectually trying to start negotiations with the Western Allies. Indeed, Ribbentrop, with both Hitler's and Himmler's approval, also had tried to scare the British and Americans into a separate peace with a common front against the Soviets by threatening to give Germany to the Russians if the peace offers were not accepted. The British finally ridiculed such proposals in mid-March. But Himmler, hospitalized, terrified of Hitler, and apprehensive of the future, tried to negotiate through the good offices of Count Folke Bernadotte, nephew of the King of Sweden and vice-chairman of the Swedish Red Cross. Although time was running out on the Nazis, Himmler thought an eleventh-hour order to stop killing the Jews who remained in captivity would placate the Western Allies into treating with him and extending favorable terms to Germany. At the same time, Himmler felt himself bound to Hitler by oath; this caused a terrible psychological block in his mind, precluding any decisive action on his part until the extreme end of the Nazi nightmare. In some vague fashion he thought Hitler's bad health would kill him during the winter or spring. Then, with a free conscience, he—Himmler —as the most powerful remaining government leader, could emerge as Germany's savior.

In practice, from the end of March until the beginning of May, Himmler was one of the most singularly ineffective personalities within the fast-diminishing Third Reich. He listened to conflicting advice, issued bloodcurdling orders against treasonous conduct, kept up his talks with the Red Cross, but remained largely in seclusion, thinking of mystically impractical courses of action that neither would nor could take place.[14]

Within the SS and in the south of Germany, conspiracies and resistance against the war multiplied and intensified. The citizens of Munich, cradle of Nazism, became restless as the war promised to close in upon them. Ernst Kaltenbrunner, Himmler's number two man, and some fellow Austrian minions within the SD were growing more concerned with sparing Austria destruction at the expense of Germany than with continuing the war. All sense of leadership was fast eroding.

Schemes and underhand plots became so entwined with the actual events of the war, which was disruptive enough, that the picture of Nazidom's last stand in the *Alpenfestung* resembled a very badly executed mosaic of mistakes rather than a mural of glorious Teutonic resistance. To many Germans it must have seemed truly that the right hand of various officials had no idea what the left hand was doing. While Karl Wolff was busy trying to throw dust in the increasingly bewildered Himmler's eyes and separately to obtain Kesselring's and Von Vietinghoff's support to surrender the forces in Italy, Himmler was spying on Wolff and attempting by his own inept diplomatic maneuvers to end the war. *Gauleiter* Hofer, by contrast, was driving hard to prepare the defenses of the Redoubt's western half for a fight. The OKW, meanwhile, was trying to oversee the southern Alpine defense line for the army in Italy and to order further surveys of sites elsewhere. During this Byzantine-like confusion Kaltenbrunner had multiple chores—some official and some self-imposed. He was spying on Wolff for Himmler, but he had other things of equal importance, too.[15]

As mentioned, Kaltenbrunner had received extraordinary powers from Himmler to administer South Germany and prepare the *Alpenfestung* in the event that the country was cut in two by the Allies. The command situation was typical of Hitler's Third Reich. The army was prohibited from taking orders from anyone save Hitler or his immediate military staff; the regional party political administrators, the *gauleiters*, would only deal directly with Hitler or Bormann. The SS was supposed to deal only with Himmler, but it was increasingly divided by competing schisms. In the case of Kaltenbrunner and Wolff, not only did Himmler have Kaltenbrunner spying on Wolff, but he also had SS General Gottlob Berger, head of the SS leadership office, watching Kaltenbrunner.

Himmler knew his own SS world well, for he suspected that Ernst Kaltenbrunner might be pursuing his own secret negotiations with the enemy. Himmler delegated enough power to Kaltenbrunner to enable him to obtain control over the local *gauleiters*. But Kaltenbrunner lacked the authority over the army necessary to make effective his mad policy of organizing the *Alpenfestung* to fight the Allies, while intending to make common cause with them against the Russians should the situation warrant. There was only one person who could grant him the power he needed. On March 23, Kaltenbrunner went to Berlin to confront his Fuehrer, Adolf Hitler.[16]

Apparently Kaltenbrunner intended to tell Hitler that the moment was at hand for the Germans to seek a deal with the Western Allies and join them against the forces of Bolshevism. He knew full well that the *Alpenfestung*, in its rickety state of readiness could not withstand any attack. Most positions were not fully ready by any means, and nothing had been done on the northern tier where the main Allied attack would probably fall.

Kaltenbrunner, however, had the idea that the Tyrol-Vorarlberg area run by Hofer could be readied in two weeks' time. He already had enlisted the aid of a few Austrian and Bavarian industrialists, one of whom supposedly had begun to install some munitions machinery in a Tyrolean cave. Furthermore, essential commodities and supplies not obtainable in the beleaguered fortress were to be smuggled in over mountain paths from Italy and Switzerland. These goods were to be paid for in counterfeit American dollars and English pounds manufactured by specialists that Kaltenbrunner had at work in Oranienburg concentration camp. Ultimately though, the whole obscure operation would fail unless Kaltenbrunner could order the army either to lay down its arms and allow the Western Allies in, or make it fight against them in the stronghold.[17]

As might be expected, face to face with Hitler, Kaltenbrunner abandoned his proposal for a premature surrender to the Americans and British. Hitler bedazzled his dull compatriot by demonstrating to him a scale model of the Austrian town of Linz which had been severely damaged. He explained that he was

60

going to rebuild it as a metropolitan center for Central Europe once the war was over. He told Kaltenbrunner that he would not be considering such plans unless he was positive that he had the means to clinch final victory even at that desperate hour. Staggered by his leader's will and apparent clairvoyance, Kaltenbrunner dropped any notion of surrender and dreamed on of an *Alpenfestung* bristling with armaments. He left Berlin and ordered his squad of expert prisoner counterfeiters transferred from Oranienburg to a camp at Ebensee in the eastern part of the Redoubt. Victory was possible; the fight would continue, but he nevertheless had to keep track of Wolff and see what was transpiring in that direction. Such was the incredibly tangled situation among the SS leadership as March ended.[18]

5

For a while in the early spring it seemed that events in the Allied camp were going to be almost as confused as those on the German side. Rumors about the Redoubt were increasing in number and intensity and Allied intelligence officers began to split into two camps: those that thought the evidence too overwhelming to ignore the Redoubt's existence, and those who felt the plethora of information on the stronghold signified extensive counterintelligence efforts by the enemy. Apparently not all intelligence personnel at SHAEF were prepared to agree with the exaggerated Seventh Army estimate. But, nonetheless, no matter where one looked—at secret sources or the civilian press—the stories multiplied.

The Swiss *Journal de Geneve* reported the training of guerrilla units under Himmler's direction, while the New York *Times'* respected SHAEF correspondent, Drew Middleton, quoted a traveler from Switzerland who had visited Vienna and who claimed that Bavaria was preparing a mountain citadel to withstand a siege of many months. To the Communist press as well as the Western Allied newspapers, the appointment of Kesselring as Von Rundstedt's successor in the West presaged a fight in the mountains. Stories of massive troop withdrawals to the Redoubt area were heard at SHAEF. Also on March 28, Eisenhower officially notified the British of his operational shift to the south and their reaction was explosively bitter.[1]

A full week had transpired since the appearance of Twelfth Army Group's Reorientation Order. Today there is mystery and confusion about the time lag between the appearance of the reorientation order and the notification to the British of the operational change. In any case Montgomery was to keep going on his narrow front until he reached Lübeck and sealed off the Danish Peninsula. To make sure Montgomery's mission was accomplished, Eisenhower offered the British commander additional troops. Montgomery at first refused, but later asked for more men, and the Supreme Commander attached Major General Matthew B. Ridgway's XVIII Corps to the British.•

The real opportunity to deal the Germans a series of lethal strokes lay with Bradley's Twelfth Army

---

• Eisenhower expressed these views in a letter to the author during the early spring of 1963.

Group in the center, which, by the end of March, held three bridgeheads across the Rhine. Bradley's aggressiveness contrasted sharply with Montgomery's caution, and to allow the former full rein, Lieutenant General William H. Simpson's American Ninth Army then attached to the Twenty-first Army Group was to be returned to the Twelfth Army Group. The British, however, were miffed at the change, puzzled over the semantics of Eisenhower's order, irritated at the manner in which the directive was announced, and dubious concerning some of SHAEF's reasons for the move.[2]

On March 27, Montgomery had confidently telegraphed the British Chief of the Imperial General Staff, Field Marshal Sir Alan Brooke, that he was ready to drive across the plains of Hannover to the Elbe River and on to Berlin. Thanks to the defeat of the Germans in the Rhineland campaign and the continuing envelopment of the Ruhr, enemy resistance was sporadic. Their mobility was gone because of Allied air superiority and their morale was disintegrating. By contrast, in the east and southeast, the Germans were still putting up stiff opposition to the Soviets before Berlin and Vienna. Montgomery, as usual, was sanguine. Suddenly, the next day and with no apparent warning to the Commander in Chief of the British forces or to the Combined Chiefs of Staff, Eisenhower informed Generalissimo Josef Stalin of the new strategy that would leave Berlin to the Russians and shift the

Western attack south. The information was then delivered to the Combined Chiefs of Staff and later to Montgomery.[3]

The British were irate that Stalin was informed before they were and felt that the Supreme Commander had exceeded his authority by dealing directly with Stalin on a question of major strategy for which the Combined Chiefs were responsible. They considered the purpose of the war to be the attainment of political goals of which Berlin was a prime one. Moreover, the message to the Russian leader seemed very obscure in detail, so that the military value of the plan could not be evaluated. The British further resented the downgrading of their role; and finally, the British intelligence service was not at all impressed by the so-called evidence of the Redoubt's existence. Eisenhower had telegraphed Stalin that after he had encircled the Ruhr, his next objective would be to divide the remaining German forces by linking up with the Russians in the Erfurt-Leipzig-Dresden axis for the following reasons:

> . . . I believe, moreover, that this is the area to which main German Governmental Departments are being moved. It is along this axis that I propose to make my main effort.
>
> In addition, as soon as the situation allows, a secondary advance will be made to effect a junction with your forces in the area of Regensburg-Linz, thereby preventing the consolidation of German resistance in the Redoubt in Southern Germany. . . .[4]

65

There was a great deal of misunderstanding concerning the affair. Perhaps basic to the problem were the questions of prestige and Anglo-American communications. The British apparently had not realized at the end of February that Eisenhower, in his own mind at least, had left open the possibility of swinging south if he felt a new set of circumstances made such a move feasible. Then, too, by the last year of the war, American preponderance of manpower and material seemed to give them initiative in questions of military policy. And there was no doubt, as well, that the Americans, especially those in the Twelfth Army Group, were still smarting over British criticism of Bradley's role in the initial stages of the Battle of the Bulge. There seemed to be a strong desire to prove the British wrong and refurbish Bradley's reputation.[*]

[*] In December, 1944, Eisenhower ordered Bradley to turn the United States First Army, under Lieutenant General Courtney Hodges, and the Ninth Army, under General Simpson, over to Montgomery during the "Battle of the Bulge." Bradley wanted the shift to be temporary and claims SHAEF said it would be. His other objection was "the question of face," for, as Bradley wrote in 1950, unless it was made clear that the change was temporary "it could be interpreted as a loss of confidence by Eisenhower in me—or more significantly in the American command." If the inference was drawn that the British "bailed out" the Americans, "the damage could be irreparable to our future role in the war." Two things did result from the command shift. Montgomery, in Bradley's eyes, "could not resist this chance to tweak our Yankee noses." Even Montgomery's Chief of Staff, Major General Sir Francis "Freddy" de Guingand, writes Bradley, "was later to chide Montgomery for the manner in which he behaved." Bradley was outraged by an interview on January 9, 1945, by Montgomery.

The Supreme Commander himself seemed to indicate this mood by his praise of Bradley's boldness, which stood out in relief to Montgomery's conservatism. On the other hand, the British Twenty-first

The Field Marshal had intended his press conference to refute British press criticisms of Generals Eisenhower, Hodges, and Bradley. The tone of the interview, however, was very condescending and it enraged the Americans, leaving a permanent scar. See, Sir Francis de Guingand, *Operation Victory* (New York, 1947), pp. 433–434. Also, although Hodges First Army was returned to Bradley's Twelfth Army Group following the Ardennes battle, the Ninth Army remained with the British until after Bradley crossed the Rhine and when that army reverted to American hands, it caused much confusion. The British apparently thought it should stay with them for their projected northern drive. When the time came to exploit the Remagen bridgehead in March, Bradley was irritated that SHAEF could not visualize its possibilities at once, but instead appeared to vacillate between his coup and the original plan whereby Montgomery would cross the Rhine north of the Ruhr with most of the Allied weight behind him. Bradley recalls that SHAEF's staff was "British-dominated" and that it "so favored the Montgomery" plan that there was no place in their thinking for the Remagen bridgehead. For other bitter criticism of Montgomery from Twelfth Army Group personnel, see Ralph Ingersoll, *Top Secret* (New York, 1946). Ingersoll was attached to Patton's Third Army. It was hard to say which Patton disliked most— Montgomery or Eisenhower's staff at SHAEF. When Bradley finally was allowed to exploit the Remagen bridgehead, and when Patton with little preparation, also sneaked across the Rhine, leaving Montgomery behind making elaborate preparations for his assault in the north, Patton and Bradley both delightedly felt they had scored one up on the British commander. Twenty-first Army Group felt SHAEF was under the undue influence of Bradley and Patton. Forrest Pogue, the most knowledgeable American military historian who has written about SHAEF, says that Montgomery's press interview still irritated Bradley in March. See, Pogue, *The Supreme Command*, p. 435.

Army Group's Headquarters, including Montgomery, was convinced that the proposed swing to the south primarily afforded the Americans the opportunity to rehabilitate Bradley's stature after the Ardennes.[5] The question of British prestige was also on Prime Minister Churchill's mind when he sent inquiries to both Washington and to SHAEF, asking for clarification of Eisenhower's new orders.[6]

The British also were apparently unaware that Eisenhower and Bradley had examined the change of operations in detail between the period of March 7 and March 21. As the British historian John Ehrman was to state later, from a purely military point of view, the Eisenhower-Bradley decision was based upon "a reasoned case," but the Supreme Commander's telegram informing the Soviets of his intentions had not stated the situation clearly enough for the British. Additional explanation was needed and in due course Eisenhower supplied it. The British grudgingly acquiesced, with Churchill and Brooke finally admitting that the shift of attack was not quite as major a change as it first appeared. But both, Brooke bluntly and Churchill tactfully if forcefully, decried the fact that American power now relegated Britain to an increasingly secondary role. As the Chief of Imperial Staff wrote in his diary, the changes were due to American "national aspirations and designed to ensure that the U.S. effort" would not "be lost under British command." The contretemps continued well into April with two issues never wholly cleared up: the fate of Berlin and Prague and the chimera of the Redoubt.[7]

6

British-Russian relations were deteriorating in 1945 because of Soviet duplicity in regard to affairs in Poland. The British believed this fact had been overlooked by Eisenhower at SHAEF. Churchill and his government were less concerned about the military merits of Eisenhower's shift to the south than were the members of the British Chiefs of Staff, but they were greatly perturbed about the increasing Russian dominance of Eastern Europe. Not to have the Western Allies as far to the east as possible when the war ended would, in Churchill's opinion, allow the Communists to pose as the primary liberators of Nazi-occupied territory.

The speed with which Stalin agreed to the Supreme Commander's strategy hardened British suspicions about Soviet intentions. The Russian dictator agreed with Eisenhower that Berlin had lost its strategic importance and he maintained he was allotting only secondary forces for its capture. As Churchill pithily observed, "This statement was not borne out by events." The American Chiefs of Staff, in answering the British objections, somewhat testily supported Eisenhower's decision, maintaining that it was in line with strategy already agreed upon, and that the Supreme Commander was within his rights in dealing directly with Stalin, as head of the Russian armed forces, not as chief of state. The British also had felt that the United States Chiefs of Staff tended to downgrade the efforts of Twenty-first Army Group and only Roosevelt's, Churchill's, and Eisenhower's personal reassurances to each other officially ended that part of the dispute.[1]

Eisenhower, Bradley, Marshall, and Smith were all products of a military system which trained its leaders to pursue one goal in waging war: destruction of the enemy forces. Political objectives were secondary. Militarily such a view is unassailable, but as General Omar Bradley ruefully admitted in retropsect, ". . . As soldiers we looked naïvely on the British inclination to complicate the war with political foresight and nonmilitary objectives." Such a non-Clausewitzian view of war seemed hopelessly ingenuous to the British. To them military policies were an adjunct of diplomatic policy and were intended to secure political aims. They looked beyond the attainment of victory. As one British military analyst acidly has inquired of Eisenhower's decision: "If at the eleventh hour of war political considerations are less important than military factors, well may it be asked, *when are they more important?* And, if they are never so, then war cannot possibly be a political instrument."[2]

Not the least of the oddities surrounding this Western Allied split has been Eisenhower's sensitivity about charges of his political naïveté. He has never attempted to minimize his responsibility for the decision not to press on to Berlin and he has never retreated from his position that it was an entirely sound military move.* As to the question of his lack of political knowledge, the problem is far less clear. The short but intense Anglo-American spat revealed the Supreme Commander as not at all unmindful of international relations. He explained to Montgomery that he was cognizant of Berlin's psychological and political importance, but he was far more interested in the location of the German army. He would seek it out, but if the chance arose to take Berlin cheaply, he would avail himself of the opportunity. Montgomery** appeared to

* In his correspondence with the author, Eisenhower stuck entirely to the military factors involved. He wrote the author on March 19, 1963 to the effect that with 20/20 hindsight it might be possible to see where a better movement could have been made, but he knew of none.

** Montgomery appeared to have agreed wholeheartedly with Eisenhower's decision on April 6, but in his memoirs, he gives the impression that he did not contest the point because an argument was "useless." There had been "so much argument already on great issues," the British military leader recalled, that he believed one more dispute was fruitless. In Montgomery's opinion, it was then too late in the European war to expect the Americans to wake up to Russian intentions or be able to do much about them.

71

concur for the sake of unity, but in his mind, he retained deep doubts.[3]

It may be partially true that Eisenhower failed to see the war's end in political terms, but perhaps there were other important reasons that influenced him. Both the Supreme Commander and Bradley appeared at that time to be weighed down by the thought of needless American casualties. In view of their experience during the savage Ardennes battle only a few months before, their concern over continued German resistance after the Rhineland campaign, and their awareness of the increasing tempo of the Pacific war, both men had every reason to feel that pure military needs should govern the situation. Then, too, there was Eisenhower's own personality to consider.[4]

The man's suavity, personal charm, and public geniality cover a complex personality; he could be tough, perhaps even ruthless, in running his staff and exercising his command responsibilities.* Most persons who have studied Eisenhower's career or who have served with him, however, have been profoundly affected by his concern for basic concepts of morality. For Eisen-

* This observation comes from Churchill's chief of staff of the Military Wing of the British War Cabinet Secretariat, General Lord Ismay. K.G. Ismay, unlike many British critics of Eisenhower, was most generous in appraising his military abilities. While he noted that the Supreme Commander could be ruthless if necessary to get a job done, he regarded criticism over Eisenhower's generalship as pointless carping. He thus summed up his beliefs: "What might have happened is speculation; what did happen was overwhelming victory."

hower morality has often been an all-embracing term covering codes of personal behavior. As is well known, he was reared in a strongly religious, pietistic family environment and this may have had considerable influence upon his military career. He once stated that at the war's beginning, too few officers concerned themselves with "subjects that touched the human soul: aspirations, ideals, men's beliefs, affection, hatred." He seems to have been affronted in both a professional and personal sense by useless destruction and noted at the end of the war that "wishful thinking" on his part led him to hope that universal fear of atomic war might bring peace where "statesmanship and religion" had failed.[5]

He was baffled and disgusted by the Nazi resistance after the Rhineland campaign because ultimately it would produce nothing save continued death and ruin. Several times, he noted, the Germans committed stupid tactical mistakes which, in his opinion, were not due to military reasons but to the perversity of the top Nazi command. Eisenhower referred to this phenomenon as the "conqueror complex," which attempted to cover the "rotten foundation" of the Nazi myth of invincibility. Hitler's madly nihilistic fight from January to his death was "tragic" to the Supreme Commander, as it visited wholesale death on Germans as well as their enemies.

Eisenhower's professional training reinforced his moral repugnance at the thought of continued slaughter. As expressed by his chief of staff, General

Smith, "Our task was to end the war swiftly and conclusively." Eisenhower, according to Smith, had but one inflexible aim in regard to all plans, decisions, and purposes of the Western Allied command and that was to destroy the German forces completely in the shortest possible time. Berlin was a terrain objective "empty of meaning" and, said Smith, Eisenhower felt that a campaign to seize it would have importance only for headlines. Too many lives were at stake.[6]

The interaction of Eisenhower's professional training with his ethical concepts may partially help to account for those decisions he regarded as strictly military, but which actually had broad political ramifications. In his book, *Crusade in Europe*, which appeared in 1948, Eisenhower speaks of Berlin, Prague, the sealing off of the Danish Peninsula and the conquest of the Redoubt in terms of strategic military value alone. One reads that the Supreme Commander's main concern was either the outright destruction or the immobilization of the German forces in those areas. Although he knew of the future occupation zones of Germany, such political divisions did not affect his military plans for conquest. Yet, recently Eisenhower recalled that one reason he urged speed on Montgomery's northern drive was to save Denmark from the Russians, and the main purpose in swinging a column to the south was to seize as much territory as possible in Austria, since the Allied political agreements about that country had not been settled.[7]

It is true, in regard to Denmark, that Eisenhower apparently was fully as determined as the British to keep the Russians out of the peninsula area. In fact, his growing impatience with Montgomery's slowness, as the spring offensives unfolded, was in part based upon the fact that he feared Soviet penetration there. The Red army, in his opinion, had been allowed to seize quite unnecessarily, if temporarily, the Danish island of Bornholm. In this particular case Eisenhower displayed the political sensitivity and foresight his critics often claim he lacked. In regard to the southern drive, however, Eisenhower stands on less sound ground.[8]

Today the former Supreme Commander reminisces that, given the nature of the occupational zones, once his central forces under Bradley made contact with the Russians, two moves were necessary: the isolation of Denmark and seizure of as much of Austria as possible to bring it under Western control. Simultaneously, the Americans were to overrun the Redoubt area where guerrilla resistance was expected. While the Redoubt matter "was kept in sight all the time . . . it was by no means the controlling factor in our planning."[9]

Actually, as April began, there was contention between the American government and the Soviets over whether or not the northwest area of Austria should be under the Russians or the Americans. Originally, until only four months earlier, the United States had wanted no occupation zones for itself at all in Austria save within the city of Vienna. And the Joint Chiefs of Staff looked with disfavor upon any sudden race against the Russians for Vienna. The dispute dragged on during April and early May with the Russians occupying Vienna and setting up the Provisional Renner

75

Government, a move which surprised and further irritated the British and Americans. The upshot of the argument was that general zones of occupation ultimately were worked out more or less satisfactorily.

But it was the British who, even while agreeing to zones, had not wished to be operationally restricted vis à vis the Russians. Churchill, not Eisenhower, had urged that the Western Allies occupy as much of Austria as possible and that they be allowed to keep their troops in tactical position until Soviet intentions about Austria and occupied Germany were made clear. He did not want local Russian military commanders pushing British or American troops out of any area. If there were to be any adjustments of such a type, they were to be settled between governments.[10]

Upon receipt of Churchill's views in April, Eisenhower once more complained about the British proclivity for mixing politics and military affairs.* Citing the precedence he had created by keeping the Russians out of Denmark, the Supreme Commander wrote General Marshall that he had initiated a formula whereby if the Russians should have arrived in Denmark before the British did, all SHAEF had to do was to request them to get out, the assumption being that they would. Speaking of Austria, he went on to say that the only area the Western Allies were in that belonged to the Russians was held by Americans. He did not feel that the Russians would be arbitrary in

* The other grievance occurred in the wake of his March announcement of his operational shift to the south.

asking the Americans to withdraw when the two forces met. Churchill's convictions prevailed, however, and Eisenhower was directed by his superiors to look to the Combined Chiefs of Staff for approval of any military withdrawals and not to civilian governmental heads. Stalin agreed to the plan in part. Churchill had carried the point, but he was not sanguine for the future. He felt that Russian intentions had to be fully ascertained before American units in Europe had been weakened by withdrawals to the Pacific and the Soviets were then freer to act.[11]

The political nuances attached to the occupation of Berlin and Austria were parts of the package of disagreements between the British and their American cousins. Also, there was the question of the Redoubt; most British leaders believed it was a chimera. So did some Americans, but others were convinced it was too big a risk to ignore. However much the Redoubt has subsequently been downgraded, in the days before Bradley's and Devers' forces overran Bavaria and Austria, it was considered very important. There was a curious dichotomy of thought and appreciation of the fabled mountain bastion as the month of April progressed.

On March 27, General Marshall had communicated to SHAEF that he, too, felt the possibility of the existence of the Redoubt warranted a drive south to cut off enemy forces from entering the area. The British intelligence disagreed with those Americans who felt that the Germans had serious intentions and capabilities

77

regarding the Redoubt. While admitting that various German ministerial departments had been observed moving south, and while acknowledging that a mountain-type *Götterdämmerung* held appeal for a few fanatics, the British considered the *Alpenfestung* to be improbable.

First of all, they reasoned that whereas the creation of the Redoubt once had been possible, by late winter and early spring Allied air domination made any such move a virtual impossibility. Secondly, the British decided that the area that supposedly comprised the stronghold could not long support a large military force plus governmental administrative sections. Finally, there was a psychological factor connected with the increasing breakdown of German resistance. The British noticed that those names most associated with the Redoubt were persons they considered to be unsuited in temperament and technical ability for such a task.[12]

Most of the allegedly important people known to be in the Alpine stronghold were the families of Nazi officials trying to conserve themselves and their material possessions. As nearly as could be ascertained in the weeks before April, the only truly important official or leader who was in the area was Goering. The tales of Himmler's command of the Redoubt were unsubstantiated. All things considered, the British did not believe in the existence of an effective Redoubt or the possibility of prolonged guerrilla activity. Eisenhower's sweep to the south seemed a wild chase that dissipated strength.[13]

Indeed, the sweep—wild or not—was at least becoming a chase of epic proportions. By April 1, elements of the First and Third American armies were advancing thirty miles a day and the Ruhr was surrounded as the Ninth and First armies met at Lippstadt. By April 4, the eastward drive that would see Germany's complete defeat began. The German command system was almost inoperative. Not only did the various headquarters lose contact and control of subordinate units, but Adolf Hitler's orders added deathly confusion to the dissolution of his armies. Always the directives read to stand and fight to the death. As Eisenhower later noted, the result was needless tragedy for thousands of Germans as well as Americans and British. More cracks in the structure of the Nazi Third Reich appeared as the Western Allies applied pressure. Other fissures manifested themselves within the Allied camp as the East and West increasingly collided over political affairs.[14]

By April the proposed surrender of the Germans in Italy once again bobbed up with a nasty reaction from Stalin. The reason was that Wolff had got Von Vietinghoff to agree to a surrender in Italy. At this point, Stalin either heard of the negotiations or noted Wolff's suspicious visits to Kesselring. Whatever happened to impress the Soviet leader, on April 3, Stalin sent Roosevelt an inflamed note about the Wolff

79

episode, charging that the Western Allies were hatching a secret plot to stop the fight in the west and to continue it in the east.

Earlier he had written to Eisenhower that three German divisions had been released from Italy for duty on the Eastern front. Given the distorted state of the Russian leader's mind, perhaps his dark doubts seemed reasonable. As noted, many Germans in high places were indeed talking of seeking accord with the west or at least splitting the Allies asunder in hopes of negotiating separately. And certainly some of these plans evolved around utilization of the *Alpenfestung*. Stalin was sure that there was collusion between the Western Allies and the Germans because, as he noted, it seemed curious that the Western front was collapsing so easily in early April while the fighting in the east remained intense.[15]

By April 9, the Russian leader's fears appeared to have some basis in fact. Wolff sent out some obscure feelers to Alexander, suggesting that an arrangement be concluded whereby German troops could be shifted to the Eastern front. Alexander refused any such move and sent word to Wolff through the OSS agents in Switzerland that the Allies would consider capitulation, not negotiation. The conversations and intrigues continued. Stalin, however, was not mollified by Roosevelt's protestations of Anglo-American good faith. The atmosphere in the Allied camp was sour.[16]

Leading American and British officers pause during staff meetings, left to right: Sir Alan Brooke, Gen. Dwight D. Eisenhower, Field Marshal Sir Bernard L. Montgomery, Maj. Gen. John B. Anderson, unidentified officer, and Lt. Gen. Omar N. Bradley.

US Army Photograph

US Army Photograph

Gen. George C. Marshall

US Army Photograph

Lt. Gen. Walter Bedell Smith

Gen. George S. Patton, Jr. *US Army Photograph*

Lt. Gen. Alexander M. Patch *US Army Photograph*

US Army Photograph   *US Army Photograph*

Maj. Gen. Sir Kenneth W.D.   Lt. Gen. Omar N. Bradley talks with Sir Alan Brooke, Chief of
Strong (British Army), G-2 SHAEF.   Imperial Staff.

Hitler's "Eagle Nest" high in the Bavarian Alps, Berchtesgaden, Germany   *US Army Photograph*

US Army Photograph

Advancing tanks of the US Third Army at Gallneukirchen with German prisoners in the background.

6th Armored Division of the US Third Army capturing Oberdorla, Germany

US Army Photograph

US Army Photograph

German barracks at Bad Tölz, later headquarters of the American 1st Infantry Division

US Army Photograph

A Sixth Army Group convoy enroute to Zell-Am-See, Austria.

German soldiers surrender their arms near Landeck
US Army Photograph

Seventh Army soldiers capture Dachau.
Men on the ground feign death after the Americans fired a volley at fleeing SS men.

US Army Photograph

Cheering prisoners at Dachau greet their American liberators.

US Army Photograph

Long lines of German and Hungarian prisoners taken by the Third Army

Lt. Gen. Alexander M. Patch meets Field Marshal Gerd von Rundstedt (center) and his son, Lt. Hans von Rundstedt.

US Army Photograph

Lt. Gen. Hermann Foertsch, Commander of 1st German Army (center), and personal representative of Field Marshal Albert von Kesselring, and his officers surrendering to Gen. Jacob L. Devers.

Hermann Goering arriving for detention camp

Field Marshal Ferdinand Schoerner after capture by forces of the 42nd Infantry Division.

US Army Photograph

Gen. Wolff in an Allied internment camp

Assistant Secretary of War Howard C. Petersen (left) congratulates Allen W. Dulles after presenting him the Medal of Merit. *US Army Photograph*

Collapse

Part 3

7

Within German circles, affairs were becoming, if possible, more divisive than ever. As the ineffectual Himmler figuratively wrung his hands while engulfed by disaster that swamped his nation, Kaltenbrunner and Wolff fought for control within the SS hierarchy. In Berlin, Goebbels began to release dismaying propaganda blasts about the Werewolves, and Himmler's *Das Schwarze Korps*, an illustrated weekly published for the SS, predicted an "absolute collapse," but stated that the German populace should continue the fight nonetheless. The immediate members of Hitler's entourage were beginning to be apprehensive.

In early April, Martin Bormann noted in his diary that if the situation became more critical, women and children were to be evacuated to the Tyrol. He could not be certain the situation would arise, but it was best to be prepared. There was no mention, however, of an *Alpenfestung* from Bormann.

Primarily, noncombatants had been the ones making their way south. No organized withdrawal had taken place. If the Redoubt truly was to be taken seriously by the Germans, no less than the Allies, it needed one prime figure—Adolf Hitler. But the Fuehrer had not yet decided to retreat to the south.[1]

Preparations by the Germans in the *Alpenfestung* limped along in April. The southern positions being in a relatively good state of readiness, most of the work was being done under Hofer's direction in the west and northwest. The northern projected line from Bregenz to about the vicinity of Gmunden to the east was defenseless. Partial fortifications, however, were about all that were being constructed anywhere within the fortress, but if even these could be manned by good troops, they might prove very dangerous to any attackers.

By mid-April Hofer was becoming increasingly fearful of attacks from all sides. At first, he was concerned primarily with the American Sixth Army Group's attacks from the west and northwest; by April 9, he felt menaced by the Russian penetration of lower Austria and he gave orders to start blocking off the eastern frontiers of the Tyrol toward Salzburg. Whatever happened to the rest of the area, Hofer meant his beloved Tyrol to be defended.

In the western section only about three-quarters of the light and heavy machine-gun nests were completed and one-third of the observation posts and tank obstacles emplaced. But the positions were skillfully sited. Labor was in short supply and it was of an extremely low quality with the greater percentage of workers being women. Still, administrative staffs from the High Command of the Army and OKW were beginning to filter into the Alpine refuge. A small operations staff was to remain in Berlin until the last minute and then depart for the south, but this plan never materialized, owing to the rapid advance of the Western Allies and the inner turmoil of Adolf Hitler's mind near the end of April.[2]

As a result of those stories planted by the SD about the *Alpenfestung*, large numbers of German soldiers, no less than their enemies, were beginning honestly to believe the rumors to be true. Many officers desperately sought to conserve their units and retreat into the Alpine region in the expectation of finding prepared defenses or even miraculous wonder weapons which might avert defeat. In this respect, the myth of the *Alpenfestung* proved to be a far crueler hoax for German soldiers than for the Allies. As nearly as can be ascertained, few, if any of Germany's top generals had heard of the National Redoubt or if they had heard of it, only a bare handful believed in it.[3]

General Franz Halder, Chief of Staff from 1938 until removed by Hitler in 1942, called the Alpine stronghold "a phantom." Nothing was assembled there, he recalls, and even if a minimum of supplies had been collected, the idea of the army hiding there, waiting an

Allied falling out, was but "cheap irony." Halder was disgusted with any professionals who believed in the fortress because their experience should have made them immune to such nonsense. No less caustic was Lieutenant General Siegfried Westphal, then fighting in the west under Kesselring, and a longtime critic of the Nazi Party and especially of Himmler. When Westphal heard rumors of the *Alpenfestung*, he refused to take them seriously. A battle by masses of troops in narrow mountain terrain without adequate air cover, without supplies, and without an extensive road network, was condemned to failure from the start, it seemed to him. The fact that the Americans took the idea seriously at all "astonished" the general. Nor was the famed mountain fighter Kesselring any believer in the *Alpenfestung* as the smashing Allied victories of April followed one after the other. To Kesselring, the Alpine Fortress made no sense as an end in itself, but only as a means to an end, to wit: a base for a strong force composed of all arms including air, capable not only of pinning down the enemy but of destroying him.[4]

The fact was, however, that as April progressed, battered German units from all of the shrinking fronts began to drift into the Alpine area. Some believed in the myth of the stronghold; most simply were squeezed into the region by the pressures of the Allied offensives.

Kesselring, for one, states that he did not share Hitler's and the OKW's fatuous belief that the Western Allies, fearful of the Communists, would move to the east and establish a common front against the Soviets.[5] What Kesselring had decided was that time had to be gained so that troops serving on the Eastern front could fight their way westward into the Anglo-American zones rather than face Russian captivity, a view adopted at the last minute by the OKW. The threat of being taken prisoner by the Communists made the German soldier tremble, according to Kesselring. His plan was to use the Alpine *massif* (as opposed to the legendary *Alpenfestung*) as a rallying point for German Army Groups Southwest, and Southeast, Army Group G and some parts of Army Group South. Once established in the mountainous territory, they could hold out until the eastern army groups escaped the Russians, retreated into the arms of the Western Allies, and surrendered.

There was no thought on Kesselring's part of attempting to use the Redoubt as some of the die-hard Nazis and various American intelligence sources thought it could be employed. Kesselring intended only to utilize mountain terrain for a delaying action. Prolonged fighting, guerrilla activities, and all similar ideas that had seized the imaginations of so many others on both sides aroused Albert Kesselring's disdain. Yet the very fact that the mountain warfare expert of the Italian campaign was, by mid-April, in a position to command troops in the south seemed ominous to some Allied observers.[6]

There was no unanimity of opinion regarding the supposed last stand of Nazidom in the mountains as the

87

end drew near. Most civilian correspondents took any bits of information about the Redoubt at face value. In the United States a twenty-seven-page news report concerned solely with the *Alpenfestung* was offered for sale at $3.00 per copy. It contained the usual figures based upon the increasingly frenetic stories coming out of both Switzerland and Germany: forty SS divisions in the Alpine citadel consisting of 200,000 men specially trained in mountain warfare; all the leading SS and Nazi party leaders would fight to the death in the Alps because capture meant death as war criminals; the fortress was designed to hold out for five years. At SHAEF the New York *Times'* correspondent, Drew Middleton, reported that stories at Supreme Headquarters told how the National Redoubt was supposedly more strongly fortified than Monte Cassino had been. The fact that the Western Allies were encountering few SS units in the field indicated that such organizations had been withdrawn to the fortress.[7]

At SHAEF, in early April, evaluations of the enemy's intentions and capabilities were professionally pessimistic although the actual results of the vast Ruhr envelopment should have indicated cause for optimism. OKW no longer controlled the situation, reserves were exhausted and communications breaking down. New German formations kept appearing, but they were the scrapings of the barrel. Yet SHAEF, in the words of General Smith, felt that this ". . . mass of manpower, ill-trained and ill-assorted as much of it was, held the possibility of prolonged resistance, particularly if it could gain the crags and canyons in the south, the site of the National Redoubt." When the Eastern and Western Allies met, SHAEF estimated, approximately 50 divisions would be left in the north and in the south, about 100, the latter the bulk of the German armor and SS units. The Redoubt had to be seized before its defenses could be fully utilized by these formations. Anti-aircraft installations were being increased and reconnaissance photographs showed that bunkers were being built around Berchtesgaden, but they were not completed in early April. The defense system, however, did not, in the opinion of Smith, seem to follow any well-defined pattern.[8]

The fact that there was little pattern of defense bothered others as well as the exasperated British. The OSS, having infiltrated the area, was not regarding the Alpine fortress with undue alarm. Dulles, in Switzerland, received many reports on the Redoubt, but he did not take them too seriously, either. He felt that Hitler was mad enough to repair to Berchtesgaden, but he also estimated that the Nazis could not put up any prolonged resistance there and so continued to concentrate on the details of the German surrender in Italy, which would preclude use of the Redoubt.[9]

Across the Atlantic in Washington, the same perplexity manifested itself. General Marshall definitely believed that a fight might take place in the Alps and he drew this conclusion to Eisenhower's attention several times. Within G-2 and the OSS in the nation's capital there was no complete agreement on the Re-

89

doubt. As nearly as can be ascertained, G-2 was split over the possibility of prolonged fighting in the stronghold. In the OSS there was a general tendency to adopt Dulles' viewpoint. On one occasion a high-ranking Army G-2 officer and member of the OSS fell into a conversation about the National Redoubt. The OSS official and the G-2 made an impromptu exercise out of the problem of what the United States Army would do if the Nazis had, indeed, established their *Alpenfestung*. Upon analysis, it seemed to both men that the whole idea was not feasible at that time and that, moreover, it was a pack of foolishness.* Both experts felt that, if through some miracle the Germans did manage to hole up in the mountains, they could not withstand the type of assault that could be launched by the powerful Allied armies.[10]

On April 11, the day before President Roosevelt died, the question of both Berlin and the Redoubt came forth once again as Simpson's Ninth Army reached the Elbe River at Magdeburg. By the fourteenth they had established a firm bridgehead. Simpson suggested to Bradley that he might be allowed to drive on to Berlin, but the Twelfth Army Group commander ordered him to wait on the Elbe. Bradley, as stated earlier, was against a drive to Berlin and so advised Eisenhower. The Supreme Commander, in turn, ordered the troops north toward Lübeck and southward in the direction of the National Redoubt. Eisenhower duly informed

* The incident of the Army G-2 officer and the Redoubt war game was told to the author in a letter by a former OSS official who must remain anonymous.

Washington and the Combined Chiefs of Staff of his decision, stating that both of those objectives were far more important than seizing Berlin. The Combined Chiefs did not dispute the move and left the responsibility to the Supreme Commander.[11]

In a sense, Bradley's central thrust had been almost too successful. Simpson was only sixty miles from Berlin and the Ninth, First, and Third Armies of the Twelfth Army Group had measured their advances at well over one hundred miles each. The Supreme Commander felt that his central armies had outrun their logistical support and that major German forces were still operating on his flanks, which had to be cleared.[12]

The Redoubt again figured prominently in Eisenhower's and Bradley's thinking. The Supreme Commander was still worried that any last stand would prolong the fighting. The two areas where this was a possibility were in the National Redoubt to the south and Norway to the north. Time was of the essence. Winter operations in the Redoubt, Eisenhower called "most laborious" and those in Norway "almost impracticable." Norway could be approached only through Denmark, so operations to gain the peninsula had to be conducted as early as possible—hence the thrust to Lübeck and Kiel as a preliminary. If, however, the National Redoubt could be reduced rapidly, that might limit the efficiency of the German defense of Scandanavia and might even bring about a surrender there.

The best way to halt the National Redoubt's effectiveness would be to link with the Russian drive in the Danube valley. Even if the Soviets and the Americans joined, the Redoubt still might be established. Therefore, the Supreme Commander decided, it would be the Western Allied aim to break into the National Redoubt area as rapidly as possible to forestall any attempts by the Germans to man their defenses effectively. Given the importance of the operations to the north and in the south, Eisenhower stated that "operations to take Berlin will have to take second place." The pertinent orders were issued to all commands on April 15.[13]

The British again protested, but on April 17 Churchill reluctantly agreed. The Prime Minister was worried about more than just Berlin. He was fearful that Bradley's drive might divert support from Montgomery and thus open the North German ports and Denmark to the Russians. It was then that he suggested to the new American President, Harry Truman, that the Anglo-American force meet the Soviets as far to the east as possible irrespective of who occupied whose zone. The British Prime Minister was increasingly skeptical of many Soviet intentions. He felt, for instance, that, since the Russians were to occupy most of the food-producing areas of Germany, the Western Allies alone would be forced to feed the starving people of Western Germany. Churchill, and his foreign secretary, Anthony Eden, also believed that Lieutenant General George Patton's United States Third Army should be allowed to drive on into Czechoslovakia and take Prague, the capital. Truman and Churchill exchanged messages until April 21, but the President supported his predecessor's belief that tactical deployment of troops in the field must remain Eisenhower's responsibility and be based upon his judgment.

Increasingly, the Supreme Commander had to make tactical decisions that affected supposed friends as well as enemies. In the east a heavy Russian drive had broken the Oder and Neisse rivers defense lines and the Red army was in Berlin's outskirts and also pushing hard on Dresden by April 21. In Italy the final Allied drive began on April 14 and its initial successes augured well for the future. At SHAEF, meanwhile, G-2 was beginning to cast its traditionally gloomy restraint aside as, from mid-April on, the combined Allied offenses picked up momentum. Now Eisenhower's intelligence officers saw the Redoubt with more clarity.[14]

As SHAEF's G-2 evaluated the situation only Nazi fanatics could not countenance defeat and their sole hope was that a protracted struggle against the Redoubt might produce Allied disunity. By April 16 and 17, G-2 reported that valid information on the National Redoubt did not establish with any certainty the enemy's intention to hold out there, but that its threat was important enough to lend validity to the idea.*

* The idea of guerrilla warfare increasingly concerned the Western Allies after they crossed the Rhine. Part of this excitement was due to Goebbels' misleading propaganda about the Werewolves. Twelfth Army Group's intelligence thought it detected "elaborate plans" for underground activity in March even when "no major operations" were then "obvious." See, Twelfth Army Group, *Report of Operations (Final After Action Reports)*, III, 220–230. However, Germany proved to be the only occupied nation of Europe in World War II that did *not* produce an underground aimed at its conquerors.

By April 22, the Western Allies in Italy believed that the Redoubt did not "yet merit such a name in the strict military sense," but that possibly the Nazis could stage some type of resistance in the Alps. On the same date SHAEF's G-2 called the Redoubt "dubious."[15]

Others elsewhere were not viewing the *Alpenfestung* as hopefully or as accurately. A captured German officer told Third Army G-2 that he fully expected a fight in the Redoubt, since such an affair suited Hitler's mentality. When GI's of the 71 Infantry Division captured Bayreuth prior to driving on the alleged outer defenses of the National Redoubt, they felt that the fighting was near an end. But then, as they considered tales of the Alpine fortress and mountain fighting, they again grew apprehensive. In the United States, as Eisenhower gave forth the new commands to hold on the Elbe and overrun the Redoubt, the New York *Times* military analyst, Hanson Baldwin, wrote that the National Redoubt did exist in truth and for proof he cited stories from the Swiss paper *Weltwoche*. According to that journal it received its information directly from Germany and the reports added up to a heavy concentration of gun nests, flak positions, bunkers, and arms depots. There were also the usual stories of underground factories located in the mountains.[16]

As the last three weeks of the European war unfolded, the welter of allegations, rumors, and planted stories increased in number and intensity among German prisoners of war, Allied soldiers, war correspondents, and members of neutral press corps. Amid mounting confusion on the German side and a crescendo of misinformation about the Redoubt, the Allies started the last phase of their final attacks.

In addition to apprehension over his flanks, Eisenhower had become concerned about the danger of accidentally running into Soviet forces with resultant mistaken fights, and anxiety about such clashes as well as about the National Redoubt influenced tactics. The British Twenty-first Army Group, reinforced by the American XVIII Corps, was told that it could cross the Elbe to the north and move on to Lübeck. The Twelfth Army Group was to hold two of its armies on the Elbe and Mulde rivers. Then it was to stop Patton's Third Army, which had reached the Czech border, and send it down the Danube valley. The Sixth Army Group in the south would eventually attack Nuremberg, Stuttgart, and Ulm and drive on to the western part of the mountain fortress. As the various final campaigns got under way, the Associated Press in Switzerland reported that all of South Germany was in a state of panic and chaos. It was. In fact, all of Germany was in a similar state.[17]

8

In Berlin there was equivocation among the topmost Nazis and military leaders about what course of action to take in the face of the devastating Allied attacks. Early on April 20, on his fifty-sixth birthday, Hitler apparently was prepared to retreat to Obersalzburg in the south; he had already sent his servants and a forty-car caravan to the mountain refuge. The day saw a succession of officials come and go at the Fuehrer's bunker fifty feet below the surface of the old Chancellory grounds. Among them were Himmler, Bormann, Goering, and Goebbels; also Field Marshal Wilhelm Keitel, Chief of the High Command; General Alfred Jodl, Chief of Operations of the OKW; Grand Admiral Karl Doenitz, Commander in Chief of the German Navy; and Albert Speer, Minister of Armaments and War Production. Hitler was optimistic despite the fact that Germany was almost split in two, the Rus-

sians were in Vienna and about to enter Berlin's outskirts, Montgomery was about to enter Bremen and
Hamburg, the Allies in Italy had seized Bologna, and
Patton was speeding through Bavaria en route to the
eastern half of the *Alpenfestung*.[1]

The visitors brought heavy pressure to bear upon
Hitler to leave for the south before the Western Allies
linked up with the Russians. Hitler would say neither
yes nor no. He created two commands in the event
that Germany was halved: Doenitz was to be full commander for the north and Kesselring for the south unless Hitler went there himself. Temporarily, he left
the southern post open. After the conference the ex-
odus from Berlin continued. Many made their way to
Obersalzburg.[2]

The plots and tensions engendered by rapid events
increased. Albert Speer left for Hamburg. He had
been secretly issuing his own orders undermining Hitler's nihilistic directives about scorched-earth policies
in regard to German factories and public utilities.
Speer wanted them handed over to the Allies intact for
reconstruction. With mixed feelings he also recognized
the necessity for Hitler's death. If that happened,
Speer planned a radio speech in which he would im-
plore the German people to surrender and not to en-
gage in any sabotage against the Allies. Speer, by his
actions, had joined the growing list of those deserting
the Nazi cause and its leader.[3]

Himmler was still divided between fearful loyalty to
Hitler and premonitions of impending disaster. He was
being pushed by an aide to either murder Hitler or

force him from power, take over the reins of leadership, and treat with the Western Allies. Himmler listened but did nothing, save for some ineffectual last-minute moves to save a few thousand Jews from death. Although he had the chance to try to obtain Swedish intervention on Germany's behalf, he was still too terrified of Hitler to make an overt move until April 23.[4]

Two days before, on the twenty-first, Hitler had ordered an all-out attack on the Russians then in Berlin's suburbs. When the attack did not materialize, Hitler fell into a blistering rage. All had betrayed him; all had deserted him; Germany and her people did not deserve him. Others might flee from Berlin to the south, but he would stay and die among the wreckage. Keitel and Jodl protested, pointing out that the bulk of whatever troops were left could be gathered in the south and that Hitler could still escape there and command them. Kesselring and Field Marshal Ferdinand Schoerner, two of Hitler's favorites, still commanded army groups in the south and in the Sudetenland. Hitler appeared to be adamant. He would die rather than fall into Russian hands, and if others wished to negotiate with the West, perhaps they should let Goering do it. The Goebbels family, meanwhile, prepared itself for suicide.[5]

Himmler heard the news at his hospital retreat and telephoned Hitler, begging him to repair to the mountain fortress, but his plea was refused. Aides were sent to the Fuehrer's bunker; they returned with the news that all was lost in Berlin. At long last Himmler felt free of his oath to Hitler and he got in touch with Count Bernadotte. The two talked in the Swedish consulate at Lübeck about Himmler's plan to surrender in the west, while holding the German front against the Soviets. Bernadotte promised nothing, but relayed the message to the Western Allies. Himmler meanwhile moved to Schwerin to be near Doenitz' headquarters for the northern command. He considered himself Hitler's logical successor, especially since Goering mistakenly had taken at face value Hitler's words about abdicating power and allowing him to negotiate. When Goering wired Hitler that he was ready to assume his new duties, the Fuehrer considered it treason and ordered his arrest. This act left Himmler—in his own mind, at least—head of the German state.[6]

The German confusion thus became worse confounded as the end neared. In Italy, Wolff and Kaltenbrunner struggled in a power play that was to affect the proposed German surrender there. The Russians again protested the maneuvers toward surrender and Alexander, on April 23, instructed Dulles to stop the talks, but the OSS official kept the discussions alive anyway.* On April 25, the proceedings took a peculiar series of turns. On one occasion, after speaking to Dulles, Wolff was ambushed by Italian partisans and had to be rescued by an American OSS agent. By the twenty-fifth, however, Wolff had got the German

* Negotiations were not broken off by Alexander solely because of Russian objections; for the truth was that the German emissaries failed to appear again until the end of the month.

commander Von Vietinghoff to support his plan, but Kesselring suddenly returned to Italy and ordered both Wolff and Von Vietinghoff arrested. The hated Kaltenbrunner was put in Wolff's place by the Field Marshal. Wolff vowed an armed defense of his headquarters at Bolzano if his rival appeared. Kesselring's orders were not carried out because there appeared to be more clashes inside the tottering Nazi edifice than there were without.[7]

Within the *Alpenfestung*, from April 20 until May 8, when the final German surrender took place, conditions were also disorganized. Kesselring recalls that between April 20 and April 24 he received the order to defend the Alpine fortress area. The southern rim had been fortified while he was in Italy; the northern and northeast sections were still bare of effective defenses. No permanent troops were stationed there and what soldiers did congregate in the mountains were a defeated army's backwash. A defense of the area would have necessitated use of Alpine troops and Kesselring had none in the *Alpenfestung*. Also, there was no effective air cover for the fortress, nor any reserves of food. Kesselring decided, in view of the inadequacy of his defense system, to stall for time to allow the three eastern army groups under his command to retire to the Alps, hoping they could surrender to the Western Allies. He issued appropriate orders.[8]

On April 24 and 25, Kesselring, along with others, was the recipient of new orders from Hitler, given through the OKW. The substance of these new di-

100

rectives was that the German armies were to resist the Soviets as strongly as possible and that defeat in the west was by comparison relatively unimportant. The final chain of OKW's command was set. Lieutenant General of Mountain Infantry August Winter, Deputy Chief of the OKW's Operations Staff, was to establish the means to defend the south of Germany while Keitel ran the northern area plus three army groups on the Eastern front. Kesselring, who commanded the Western front, was responsible for the troops in Italy, the Balkans, Bavaria, and Austria.[9]

The proposed effect of these new orders was to create some type of connection with Berlin and hold back the Russians. The goal, naturally, was never realized as it bore no relation to actual events, but the idea of concentrating on the Russians rather than on the Anglo-American forces held obvious appeal for many Germans right to the end.

On the night of April 24, Hitler summoned Field Marshal Schoerner from Czechoslovakia to his bunker headquarters in Berlin. Despite the fact that only a few days before, Hitler had declared that all was lost and had seemed to abdicate power, by the twenty-fourth he was acting in full command again. Schoerner, nicknamed the "Bloodhound" because of his martial Teutonic qualities, received an honor from his leader that night. Hitler gave Schoerner a direct order (*Fuehrerbefel*), conferring upon him the tactical supreme command of the *Alpenfestung*. Schoerner's work in the *Alpenfestung* meant far more than merely organiz-

101

ing an Alpine front. He was to continue fighting with his army group in Bohemia, but eventually withdraw into the *Alpenfestung* where he was to keep his units intact and husband his strength until the inevitable fight erupted between the Western and Eastern Allies. At that point, the troops of his command would sally forth in common cause with the Western Allies against the Bolsheviks.*[10]

Although this direct order was to be written down, after being explained to him by Lieutenant General Hans Krebs, Chief of the General Staff of the Army, Schoerner never received the written copy. Schoerner's command, though called a tactical one, was pregnant with political implications. He did not receive any orders, however, to start fortifications on the northern or northeastern fronts. He took his verbal directory to heart and flew off to rejoin his army group in Bohemia where, upon landing, he sent back a tele-

* Schoerner, although not a Nazi Party member, was one of Hitler's favorites. He actually did not hear of the *Alpenfestung* until summoned to the *Fuehrerhauptquartier* (Fuehrer's headquarters), and as far as he knows, the idea originated with the OKW. After his capture and imprisonment by the Russians for war crimes, he was interrogated about the Redoubt and its alleged use by the Germans and the Allies against the Soviets. He served ten years in Russian captivity and was then released. In 1955–1956, the West German Federal Republic brought Schoerner to trial for alleged crimes perpetrated against troops of the German army, including summary executions of soldiers for lack of discipline. Schoerner was jailed for approximately four years by the Bonn government. At present, he lives in Munich. See, *Newsweek*, Oct. 28, 1957, p. 42.

gram to his Fuehrer urging him to join his headquarters there. Hitler refused the suggestion, but he kept Schoerner's loyalty in mind. News of the absent Himmler's overtures to the Western Allies reached Hitler and infuriated him and, along with Goering, he exiled the SS leader from the dissolving Nazi Party. He rewarded his faithful servant Schoerner in his political testament by naming the Field Marshal Commander in Chief of the German army under a government to be headed by Doenitz, in place of Himmler, after Hitler's suicide.[11]

Schoerner's plans seem quixotic today, but they were very much in vogue among the officers of the OKW, many Nazis, certain American officers, and the Russians. Schoerner was eventually captured by the Communists and tried for war crimes and at one of his Moscow trials he was interrogated about the sinister use of the *Alpenfestung*. The Russians remained convinced, according to Schoerner, that the Western Allies and the troops in the mountain citadel would join against the Soviet forces. Eisenhower, of course, did consider the Redoubt a cause for future Allied estrangement and it shaped his strategic and tactical thinking in the European war's closing days. Illusory as the *Alpenfestung* was, it had its effect.[12]

For those officers on the German side charged with the defense of the fortress, April was a desperate month. The mountain experts, Kesselring and August Winter, called upon another mountain infantryman, Lieutenant General Georg Ritter von Hengl, to take charge of the northern Alpine front on about April 20.

Von Hengl, like the engineer Marcinkiewicz, was in despair at what he was supposed to command. As a defensive system he had never heard of the *Alpenfestung* until the end of March and by the time he got into the area, the conditions were chaotic. As nearly as either Von Hengl or Marcinkiewicz could tell, the fabled underground installations consisted of a Bavarian plant, making airplane parts and located within a tunnel. And there were depots in subterranean shelters which originally had no connection with the Alpine fortress. The myths of the prized SS troops in the stronghold stood revealed as tales for the most part. There were the SS troops at Bolzano, Italy, but elsewhere Von Hengl personally could only account for the two SS battalions at Berchtesgaden plus the officers at the Bad Toelz training school.[13]

Furthermore, no full or completely equipped German army divisions had been transferred into the region. What troops there were for Von Hengl to use were only the already drained local garrisons of the Replacement Army. The quality of the men was limited. Heavy weapons and ammunition were lacking and the whole area was being inundated by thousands of noncombatant personnel from civilian ministries, the ground personnel of the *Luftwaffe*, and high-ranking military staffs without troops. By the surrender, Von Hengl estimates that 90 per cent of his troops were noncombatants. To add insult to injury, it became obvious to him that local opinion was clearly against supporting any combat operations in the *Al-*

penfestung. Overt hostility was not evident, but apathy and passivity marked the civilian populace. They wanted the war to end. None of the prerequisites necessary for guerrilla activity could exist under such conditions.[14]

The armies of the Reich were so smashed from mid-April on, that reorganization in the mountains was impossible. From Italy, from the Rhine, from the Balkans, they straggled into the Alps—but not as organized units. They were mere fragments of armies. Barely any men from Schoerner's forces in Czechoslovakia made it back to the *Alpenfestung.* As the broken and often weaponless remnants of the German army gathered in the mountains, their appearance was so disquieting to the hastily assembled Alpine defenders that the already shaky morale plummeted.• Capitulation was obviously near anytime after April 20. Yet, to some Americans the Redoubt still seemed somewhat formidable and promised more heartbreaking combat.[15]

• A Waffen SS General named Otto Hoffman gave United States interrogators a picture of the Redoubt's last days. He did not even learn of an attempt to defend the Vorarlberg, Tyrol, and Bavarian *massifs* until April 27, 1945, yet the SS allegedly was the nucleus of the defensive system. The SS General had been fighting troops of the United States Seventh Army, which had made mincemeat of the German forces as they attempted to stop the Americans and French. Hoffmann, too, points out that elements of the native population were "not reliable" and that some local militia were reported to have fired on German soldiers.

9

On April 21, at SHAEF, General Smith held an off-the-record press conference. For the record, he again went over the reasons for not driving on Berlin, but his comments on Anglo-American operations dating from April 21 were unofficial. He said that SHAEF really did not know too much about the Redoubt, nor what it would find there; but he went on to say that "We are beginning to think it will be a lot more than we will expect (*sic*)." Especially, said Smith, more extensive underground installations than originally deemed possible. Also, if either Hitler or any of his cohorts were in the National Redoubt, they might use the radio to keep resistance alive. As a consequence, to bring the war rapidly to an end, Eisenhower was sending Patton's Third Army and Lieutenant General Alexander Patch's Seventh Army into the eastern and

106

western halves respectively of the Alpine fortress on the next day. Once the Redoubt fell, according to Eisenhower and Smith, the garrisons in Denmark, Norway, and Holland would probably fall. Smith reiterated that from a purely military point of view Berlin held no significance any more, "not anything comparable to that of the so-called national redoubt and a jumping-off place from which we can later operate in Norway."[1]

To the question of how difficult the Redoubt would be to reduce, Smith said he did not think the job would be too hard. He guessed the fighting might last for about a month and be followed by guerrilla warfare for an indeterminate time. He mentioned that there was "a hell of a lot of pressure" from Washington to redeploy troops to the Pacific and this would affect the timing of victory day. Such a proclamation would have to come from the Allied governments, not Eisenhower, and he did not feel that the German government would ever surrender formally. The announcement, said Smith, could occur weeks or months before or after the Redoubt collapsed. He went on to say, in answer to questions, that the German forces in Italy could act as a natural reserve for the Redoubt, but that he did not think they would dare to use gas in its defense.[2]

Although he was rather sanguine about the future, Smith still overestimated the National Redoubt's capabilities for immediate defense and as an area for sustained guerrilla operations. Correspondent Drew Middleton of the New York *Times* came away from the news conference in an overly somber frame of mind. Writing guardedly with Smith's evaluation and forecast in mind, the newspaperman predicted that the Redoubt's reduction would be Eisenhower's major problem, perhaps necessitating a combined full-scale military campaign by both Russians and Americans.[3]

SHAEF's G-2 and the Third Army's General Patton saw the bogus fortress in a clearer light on April 22. G-2 referred to it as the "very dubious 'National Redoubt' " and stated that aerial surveillance failed to confirm any large-scale build-up of forces and positions in Bavaria. In view of its "present evidence" G-2 did not want to "overemphasize the importance" of the Redoubt. The fortress could exist if Hitler or a leading satrap were there, but G-2 stated that American forces should be able to overrun the mountain country, forestalling any occupation of defensible terrain. When this happened, the regime would fall. As Patton received orders from Bradley to shift his attack to the southeast and enter the eastern half of the *Alpenfestung*, the volatile expert on tank warfare felt it was obvious that the end of the war was very close at hand. But, he noted, ". . . there were those who insisted that a great concentration existed to the south." So, the Third Army dutifully galloped off after the ghost of the National Redoubt.[4]

The "those" to whom Patton referred may have been responsible directly to General Omar Bradley, Commander of the Twelfth Army Group. On April

24, as the Russians encircled Berlin, as Hitler read Himmler and Goering out of the Nazi Party and refused Schoerner's last appeal to escape from the doomed capital, and as Kesselring, Winter, Von Hengl, and Marcinkiewicz despairingly viewed the defeated disorder within the Alpine area, Bradley contemplated the National Redoubt and the future with the deepest pessimism.

The Twelfth Army Group's commander told visiting Congressmen that the fighting might last a month more or conceivably even a year. When the politicians looked alarmed, Bradley shared his gloomy thoughts with them. His caution was born of an "obsession with the Redoubt" caused by G-2's accounts of "a fantastic enemy plot" for the establishment of the Alpine citadel. When intelligence talked of SS units being withdrawn for the defense of the fortress, "a swift check of the battle order on both our and the Russian front revealed a suspicious concentration" of elite formations on the Western Allies' southern flanks.[5]

Later, Bradley ruefully recalled that the tales of the Redoubt "grew into such an exaggerated scheme that I am astonished we could have believed it as innocently as we did." But believe it Bradley and numerous others did at the time, and as the frank army group commander further commented, while the myth lasted "this legend of the Redoubt was too ominous a threat to be ignored and in consequence it shaped our tactical thinking during the closing weeks of the war." Bradley's apprehensions were within twenty-four hours of

109

being partially dispelled. Not that the dawning of truth seemed at the time to make any great difference to the Americans, for the attacks of Patton and Patch swept into the vacuum of the National Redoubt.[6]

Patton's forces, with Patch on their right flank, straddled the Danube, largely avoiding Czechoslovakia and involvement with the Russians in that country, and the two armies plowed forward. The GI's of the Third Army, expecting the worst from a tough inner Alpine defense line manned by the SS, were happily astonished that the peripheral positions proved to be nothing but badly manned roadblocks. Perhaps they would have been even more surprised on April 25 if they had been able to listen in as Ninth Army intelligence officers to the north interrogated Kurt Dittmar, the official radio spokesman for the German Wehrmacht. Dittmar had poled across the Elbe and surrendered to the Americans. He brought interesting news. He correctly appraised the current situation by stating that Hitler and Goebbels would stay in Berlin and die, Goering was out of favor, the war was lost, and the fabulous National Redoubt was nothing but a dream.[7]

The strings of the noose prepared by the Allies drew tighter as the Russians and Western Allies met on the Elbe at Torgau on April 26. At the same time the American Seventh Army headed for the Brenner Pass to cut off any German troops seeking entry into the southern part of the Redoubt—the only section of the fortress with effective defensive positions.

Meanwhile, Wolff's and Kaltenbrunner's confused vendetta in Italy neared an end as the three-month talks on the surrender of the German army in Italy were concluded. A document of capitulation was signed on behalf of Von Vietinghoff and Wolff at Alexander's headquarters. Kesselring, aware of what was happening, remained aloof, still bound by his oath to Hitler. The surrender was to take effect on May 2. While Wolff and Von Vietinghoff were in Wolff's headquarters at Bolzano, *Gauleiter* Franz Hofer suddenly appeared in their midst and promptly telephoned Himmler and Kesselring of what the two were doing. Himmler's reaction was pallidly devoid of reality. Querulously he asked details about Wolff's evacuating his family and setting a bad example to other SS officers. That was his only response. Kesselring, however, put pressure on Wolff to delay or abrogate the capitulation, but to no effect. The orders were issued and with Hitler's death on April 30, Kesselring, free of his oath, reluctantly backed down. Kaltenbrunner fled.[8]

10

As the Americans drove into the National Redoubt from all sides, they were in many cases hampered more by the problems of a too-rapid motorized advance than by German resistance. Units of the Seventh Army found the outer defenses "spotty and passive," but the Second SS Mountain Division fought well against the Forty-fifth Infantry Division. Generally, though, the American armored columns in the west rolled twenty to thirty miles a day. The pursuit of the Germans, in the words of the Seventh Army's *After Action Report*, was "a fantasy of violence and speed and extravagant incident." On one occasion United States tanks ran up to a camouflaged airfield and held target practice on the jet planes trying unsuccessfully to get airborne. The members of the 103rd Infantry Division were enviously astonished to flush German troops from foxholes which contained not only the surrendering soldiers but their girl friends as well. When the beaten men gave themselves up, they ran forth dragging the girls with them into captivity.[1]

Farther to the east, the Third Army's experience was much the same. Its G-2 section was never as impressed by the Redoubt as its Seventh Army counterpart had been. In fact, the Third Army rarely, if ever, mentioned the Redoubt in its plans until after mid-April. The shift to the south and its subsequent march down the Danube came as a surprise to the army's staff leadership. Although the men in the field expected the German resistance to be worse the farther they drove into the Redoubt, Third Army headquarters evaluated the situation more realistically and accurately. The army's chief job during April and May, they thought, would prove to be occupation and mopping up. By April 20, the G-2 of Patton's army decided that any plans the Germans had for moving the SS into the Redoubt could not be carried out as the bulk of the elite units were spread out and their strength dissipated. The Third Army certainly was meeting SS units, but they were scattered about the entire area and their defensive efforts were correspondingly diffused, although occasionally there were stiff fights. Often, however, the German troops were of a very low grade and once they even used five hundred women in defensive positions.[2]

Prisoner of War camps were beginning to be overrun by the Seventh and Third Armies and the joyous

113

soldiers gratefully embraced their American liberators. But other types of camps had been seized by the GI's, too, and these shocked and sobered the troops as perhaps no other sights that they had witnessed during the war.

Near Weimar in Thuringia, men of the Third Army's Eightieth Infantry Division had broken into the ghastly confines of Buchenwald concentration camps on April 11. Stunned almost beyond comprehension by the scenes that greeted them, the soldiers attempted to care for the surviving inmates. Actually, only about 21,000 persons remained, since approximately 30,000 others had been removed by their captors at the last minute. Even as the Americans started to care for the ex-prisoners, 150 of them died of malnutrition or disease after only twenty-four hours of freedom.

Sickened by what they saw, the soldiers wonderingly looked at the camp's crematoriums and unbelievingly inspected Barracks No. 61 of the hospital compound. From the outside the building appeared to be a conventional one-story barracks. Inside were two rows of four-tiered shelves, divided every five and a half feet by partitions. Each division was about a foot and a half high and it had not been uncommon for the camp's former guards to place six emaciated wrecks into each hole where they lay on their sides awaiting death. In the hospital, many had died from sadistic medical experiments. Terrible tales were to be told about Buchenwald such as those that concerned SS guard Sommer who eventually admitted to having personally killed 150 persons in one six-month period. Sommer had strangled men with his hands, crushed their heads with his boots, and caused skin to be peeled from their private parts. A former inmate of Buchenwald, Eugen Kogon, described how Sommer would kill prisoners in his room, which was decorated by an illuminated skull. After a murder, Sommer would place the body under his bed and sleep peacefully.[3]

The charnel-house scene was set near a charming area of Thuringia, and Buchenwald's nightmare contrasted evilly with the country around Weimar. The incongruity of the two adjacent communities symbolized the Germany of World War II. Weimar was the home of such revered nineteenth-century German poets as Schiller and Goethe. After World War I it had been the birthplace of Germany's first attempt at a democratic form of government—the ill-fated Weimar Republic. But there was little idealism or culture extended to Buchenwald by the Weimar of the Second World War. Its citizens knew of the camp's existence and many made a profitable living from it, selling various items to the SS and trafficking in black-market goods, much of which had been stolen from the inmates by the SS guards. The town inhabitants raised few objections to what went on in Buchenwald. As the Americans drew near, Weimar's citizens were terrified that the prisoners might break out and exact vengeance. Only by a difficult feat of self-discipline did prison leaders maintain control, fearful of a last stroke of brutal reprisal by the remaining SS guards.[4]

While the freed inmates at Buchenwald cried and cheered their liberators, thousands of its former inhabitants died of starvation and suffocation in railway cars headed for another camp named Dachau. Not until April 29 did troops from the Forty-second and Forty-fifth Infantry Divisions, attached to the United States Seventh Army, capture Dachau near Munich, Bavaria. About three hundred guards put up a fight and then fled or surrendered. Around 30,000 prisoners were liberated. Sights at Buchenwald, Ohrdruf, Landsberg, Belsen, and other horror camps were repeated at Dachau. Inmates pathetically charged the electrified enclosure wires to gain their freedom as the Americans entered the camp. They obtained weapons and began shooting and stoning their former captors, who sought GI protection. Uneasily, the Americans fired over the heads of the enraged skeletons who sought to even hideous old scores.[5]

In the western half of the Redoubt *Gauleiter* Hofer was in a frantic quandary. A Party man, and the original proponent of the Alpine fortress, he was bound to believe that a defense had to be made. The political-administrative side of his duties, however, demanded that he do something for the populace under his jurisdiction —and the public was sick of the war.

On April 28, a revolt broke out in Munich, the town described by Eisenhower as "the cradle of the Nazi beast," and another was reported at Salzburg. The one at Munich was squelched in a last brutal show of violence, but the citizens of Bavaria and Austria were evidencing definite signs of separatism and disaffection. The local militia was proving less than militant and Austrian partisans eventually aided elements of the Seventh Army to reach the Brenner Pass and affect a link-up with troops from the Italian-based Fifth Army. Retreating German troops complained that civilians made a greater demonstration of hospitality and welcome for the conquering Americans than for themselves. Furthermore, top officers within the dissolving German army rejected any thought of guerrilla warfare in the *Alpenfestung* on the grounds that such activities were militarily hopeless and invited Allied reprisals against the civil populace.[6]

While such scenes were taking place, Hofer plunged about, demanding the impossible of the German army and, to the irritation of Von Hengl, interfering in its affairs. At one point he asked for a motorized regiment to restore internal order at Bozen, but Von Hengl passed him on to Kesselring to let that hard-boiled commander deal with him. On April 30, Hofer took to the air and sowed even further confusion among the troops—if that were possible—by declaring that the fight would continue in the mountains, but that villages and farms were not to be defended. The latter proposal met with civilian favor, while the former was ignored by one and all. Hofer, in due course, was captured near his home by the Americans at Halle, Austria, on

May 2, and he was given a lengthy interrogation by intelligence officers. He admitted that the *Alpenfestung* was but a defenseless dream. Of his fifty-six militia battalions only three were left. The German author of the *Alpenfestung* never fought there, despite the compelling fantasy that had consumed his imagination and energies for eight months. With the permission of his captors, he bid his family good-by with a "Heil Hitler" and a Nazi salute.[7]

As the image of the Redoubt vanished upon close scrutiny by the Third and Seventh Armies, the familiar Anglo-American argument on how far east to meet the Russians continued. After the twenty-first of April the British regarded deployment of troops as more than ever a question of politics as well as tactics. Truman, Marshall, and the Joint Chiefs of Staff felt somewhat the reverse. Eisenhower, they reiterated, was in the best position to know where they were most needed and the decision should be his. But the British Chiefs of Staff and the Prime Minister urged the Americans to take Prague, Czechoslovakia, at least.

The taking of Western Czechoslovakia might, in Churchill's opinion, influence the postwar politics not only of that country but of adjacent ones. If the Western Allies failed to drive into Bohemia, the once-democratic state of Czechoslovakia might suffer the same fate as was befalling Yugoslavia. If the opportunity presented itself, Churchill felt that Eisenhower should allow Patton entry into Czechoslovakia to capture Prague and occupy as much as he could of the country.

The British Prime Minister added that such a projected move should not interfere with the main operations against the Germans, but he deemed it necessary, nonetheless, to have such political considerations brought to the Supreme Commander's attention.[8]

General Marshall sent Churchill's views to Eisenhower with the now famous comment: "Personally and aside from all logistic, tactical or strategical implications, I would be loath to hazard American lives for purely political purposes." As the American military historian, Forrest Pogue, has noted, "startling" as Marshall's statement appears today, it was in full accordance with United States World War II military policy. Also, as Pogue points out, Eisenhower was never given any directive to restore the balance of power in Central and Western Europe. Such planning would have exceeded the Supreme Commander's scope and responsibilities. That would have been the task of his superiors and Washington obviously outweighed London at that stage of the war. Eisenhower continued to concentrate on his basic mission as he and his staff saw it— immediate destruction of the remaining German forces and a shift of troops to the Pacific theater.[9]

The State Department, however, agreed with Churchill and told President Truman that if United States soldiers got as far as the Vltava River which ran through Prague, America would be in a better political position *vis à vis* Russia about Austrian and Czechoslovakian affairs. Eisenhower, on April 29, in commenting to Marshall about such reasoning, still was

119

determined first to obtain Lübeck to the north and reduce the ephemeral Redoubt. These must remain his priorities, although it was increasingly obvious to others including SHAEF's G-2 section that no Redoubt was in existence. Even after those goals had been met, if it still seemed desirable to move into Czechoslovakia, the Supreme Commander would not, to gain a political prize, take any action which he deemed militarily unwise unless he received orders from the Combined Chiefs of Staff. In his opinion the Red Army could reach Prague before Patton could. He was wrong in regard to the latter estimate, but he never received any orders to march on Prague.[10]

On April 30, Eisenhower informed the Russians fully of his intentions. The Soviets agreed, but on May 4, when Eisenhower indicated that he could, if it was agreeable, move farther east than the Pilsen-Karlsbad region to the vicinity of Prague, the Russians objected strenuously. Eisenhower had found that he had considerable forces from Patton's Third Army available for a move, for by May 2, elements of the Seventh Army had met troops from the Fifth Army at the Brenner Pass. When the units from Italy met with those from the north, the Redoubt truly ceased to be feasible even to the most ardent exponent of a guerrilla warfare operation. The Russians, however, had absolutely no desire to see Patton liberate Prague and have the Czechs thankful to the Americans rather than to the Soviets for their delivery. As one British critic, Chester Wilmot, remarked, Eisenhower's "eagerness" to overrun the mythical National Redoubt let slip the opportunity to seize Prague. The Russians were still about seventy miles from the city and strongly opposed by Schoerner's army group, which was holding fast and fighting desperately.[11]

The Supreme Commander allowed the Third Army to cross the Czech border and advance as far as the Pilsen-Karlsbad line agreed to by Stalin. Before the move, the Russians had told Eisenhower that if American and Russian units ran into each other on their advances, great confusion could result. Also, the Soviets sharply reminded him that they had acceded to an earlier request from the Supreme Commander that they stop their drive to the lower Elbe in North Germany. The implication was that turnabout was fair play. The chances, however, of the Russians and Americans driving headlong into each other's forces on the ground appear to have been somewhat remote in view of Schoerner's stubborn defense and the Red Army's distance from Prague.[12]

Whatever the case, Eisenhower honored the request; when the Czech underground in Prague revolted on May 5 and begged for American help, the Supreme Commander refused but passed on the pleas to the Russians. The fighting in Prague was still going on after the Germans had surrendered at Rheims on May 7. Since Schoerner's headquarters had heard the news from the underground's radio and thought it was a partisan's trick, the combat continued. Churchill urged Eisenhower not to be inhibited by his agreement

121

with the Communists if he had the forces available. Eisenhower, however, maintained his understanding with the Russians. He also sent a patrol with a German representative from Doenitz' headquarters to Schoerner and warned the Field Marshal to bring the fighting to an end or face serious consequences. The Russians entered the Czech capital on May 12, but almost three weeks passed before they allowed the Americans to come into the city. The Communist political stratagem was a success. They assumed the stance of the heroes solely responsible for Czechoslovakia's delivery from the Germans.[13]

The myth of the Redoubt was still exerting a strange magnetism even as it died. It was determining Allied and even German strategy and tactics right to the end. Rumors continued to flow and inundate headquarters and units on both sides. On April 29, the eve of Hitler's death, SHAEF heard that thousands of troops from the eastern Austrian front, from South Germany and from Italy had managed to reach the central defense zone of the Redoubt. There was also a completely inaccurate report that Himmler was in Munich. Apparently this indicated an attempt at some type of defense under SS leadership. Orders, accordingly, came from SHAEF for the Sixth Army Group G-3 to move rapidly to prevent more Germans from retiring into the fortress center. The enemy troops in the Danube valley and Czechoslovakia saw the American advances of the Seventh and Third Armies blocking their entry into their *Alpenfestung*. To the Germans failure to

122

reach it meant Russian captivity. But the Americans saw it differently. The Salzburg Pass became a focal point for Americans and Germans alike, since it remained the last northern entry into the National Redoubt and the troops of both nations aimed for it.[14]

Originally, Salzburg had been in Patton's domain, but his flanks appeared overextended and SHAEF redirected the objective instead to the care of the Seventh Army, which advanced through the disintegrating German defenses. It sent a corps each racing for Salzburg and Berchtesgaden. The latter was captured on May 5 by troops of the French Second Armored Division attached to the XXI Corps. When the Frenchmen ascended the fabled "Eagle's Nest," it was empty. There was no fanatical defense of Hitler's private retreat. The *Götterdämmerung* had taken place far to the north in Berlin. The Tri-color, with martial as well as poetic justice, rose high above the rubble-strewn heart of the mythical *Alpenfestung*.[15]

Still, even as Hitler died and Berchtesgaden was captured, the fortress continued to fascinate. Its mystique predictably attracted a certain type of Nazi. The Austrian-born SS General Otto Skorzeny, whose rescue of Benito Mussolini and similar exploits had made him one of Hitler's favorites, wandered into the area near Alt Aussee with other confirmed, if less effective Nazis, about the time that his Fuehrer died. Skorzeny had vague orders to assemble a group of Alpine defenders for partisan work, but he found the highly touted defense system and its hidden supplies to be nonexistent. Wanted by the Allies for alleged war crimes, he tried to flee Wagnerian valor in the Alps for tranquility in neutral Spain.[16]

Another mysterious visitor to the Redoubt area was Reinhard Gehlen, chief of the OKH's Foreign Armies East Department. He was in charge of anti-Soviet espionage operations. When the Russians crossed the Oder, Gehlen and his staff took as many microfilmed documents as they could and fled to the *Alpenfestung*. They hoped to be picked up by the Americans and not fall into Red hands. Gehlen was certain that the United States could use his invaluable records and services. Eventually, he was proven right,* but the Americans did not for many weeks tumble to the fact that they had such a prize. Bedazzled by the lure of grabbing top-ranking Nazis and prominent military leaders, they ignored Gehlen, much to his puzzlement. For days he sat in a mountain chalet at Elendsalm, Bavaria, impatiently awaiting capture. He would not go out. The Americans did not come up to where he was. When finally they did, further weeks went by before someone discovered what an intelligence bonanza Gehlen represented. He was perhaps the only German in the Redoubt who truly was able to use the area as a

---

* Gehlen now works just as mysteriously for the West German Federal Republic. Allegedly, his first postwar operations were subsidized by the United States C.I.A. The Soviet counterespionage services, however, infiltrated Gehlen's new organization, causing much anguish in both Bonn and Washington. Gehlen avoids any publicity and almost no photographs of him exist.

place from which to link up with the Western Allies against the Soviets.[17]

A very few SS officers, however, as late as May 2, were still galvanized by the thought of fighting in the *Alpenfestung*. By that date Hitler's suicide had been broadcast, the Seventh and Fifth Armies had joined at the Brenner Pass, the German forces in Italy had capitulated to Alexander, Berlin had just fallen, and the British had met the Russians at Wismar in the north. Even so, some SS commanders ordered their men to defend valley entrances and hillsides to block the Americans and French. Save in isolated cases the orders were not obeyed.[18]

The troops of the United States Seventh and Third Armies also remained hypnotized by the National Redoubt almost to the end. As they rapidly advanced, they kept meeting disorganized units of the German army, but rarely did they meet SS units, which were almost always kept in reserve. Yet the men in the field still kept expecting the fanatical resistance that never materialized. When troops of the American Forty-second Infantry Division found themselves following an *Autobahn* into the heart of the supposed fortress without serious opposition, it dawned on some that perhaps the fabled Redoubt was but a myth. With the capture of Landeck, Innsbruck, Salzburg, Berchtesgaden, and the Brenner Pass, the Redoubt area was increasingly blanketed by American and French troops. The Redoubt was no longer even a pretense, and complete, utter confusion marked the German operations, such as they were. Between May 3 and May 5 the bulk of the occupants within the Redoubt surrendered unconditionally to General Devers. On May 7 at SHAEF in Rheims the rest of all the German armed forces unconditionally surrendered, too.[19]

Although the Americans had become increasingly suspicious about the Redoubt's reality, it nevertheless came as a shock when Lieutenant General Hermann Foertsch, commander of the German First Army representing his Army Group G, told Devers that he had food for only six days. When asked how many men there were to feed, Foertsch said he thought between 250,000 and 350,000! Devers and his staff were astonished. Where were the caches of food and supplies? Was it possible that so many troops, jammed into the center of the Redoubt, were giving up unconditionally without a fight? Did Foertsch fully understand the demand? He did. The underground storehouses, of course, had never existed and the huge numbers of men in the Redoubt were, for the most part, whipped, demoralized and in no mood to fight at all. Sporadic fighting did continue in one case involving SS troops at Woergl on the Inn River. The Nazis attempted to recapture a castle containing important French prisoners which the original German garrison had surrendered to the Americans. When the SS attacked the castle, German troops helped repulse their own countrymen.[20]

The *Alpenfestung*, its name a mockery, yielded a rich crop of German wartime leaders. The Seventh

126

Army captured the recently retired and greatly mortified Von Rundstedt in his bath, and also Field Marshals Wilhelm List, Wilhelm Ritter von Leeb, and Kesserling. The feared mountain fighter surrendered near Berchtesgaden to Major General Maxwell D. Taylor, Commanding General, 101 Airborne Division. Nazi political personalities abounded in the area, as well. But they had gone south seeking a sanctuary rather than a place from which to fight. Among them were Robert Ley, the hard-drinking, foul-mouthed former labor minister; Julius Streicher, lecher, Jew-baiter extraordinary and editor of the anti-Semitic, pornographic newspaper *Der Stürmer*; and Ernst Kaltenbrunner, who meekly surrendered at Alt Aussee accompanied by an aide and two SS men.[21]

A huge man, standing six feet four inches, and having a scarred face, Kaltenbrunner had ineffectually tried to disguise himself by shaving off his mustache. Found in his possession were quantities of candy, much ammunition, weapons, and some of the counterfeit American money made for him by his select group of concentration-camp inmates. The former RSHA head, in spite of his denials, was positively identified when his mistress, Countess Gisela von Westrop, impulsively kissed him as he was brought into custody. Upon questioning, Kaltenbrunner talked mystically of setting up a headquarters at Alt Aussee and establishing radio contact with anti-Bolshevik underground groups all over Austria and Germany. An observer noted that the number two leader in the once-feared

SS sweated profusely in the cool Alpine breeze as he was given a preliminary grilling. Unwilling to divulge too much, the man who was to be hanged eventually for crimes against humanity was reported to have trembled visibly when his captors implied that unless he talked freely to them, he might be turned over to others possessed of less sensitive scruples.[22]

With Hitler and Goebbels dead in Berlin, there remained but two more of the quartet that had presided over the Nazi movement and the Third Reich. Logically, according to the American theory, they had to be in the Redoubt, providing the leadership for the expected Nazi guerrilla forces. These two were Goering and Himmler. The former had long been within the *Alpenfestung; Luftwaffe* headquarters had been operating from Berchtesgaden in the war's closing weeks. After his fall from power, Goering remained in the south and at the end he was under house arrest by the SS. He did not, however, live up to his earlier statement to Kesselring that he would die a hero's death there. Quite the contrary. On May 9, he surrendered to Major General J. A. Dahlquist, commanding general of the Thirty-sixth Infantry Division. Such was Goering's bluff charm that he was treated with cordiality by his captors. When SHAEF heard of such cases of bonhomie with former Nazis, it snappily reminded one and all that such fraternization was expressly forbidden by the Supreme Commander. Goering, stripped of his medals, went off to imprisonment and eventually death by suicide in a prison cell.[23]

Well after the general surrender, the Third Reich's most-wanted and hated man aimlessly and indecisively strayed about North Germany. Heinrich Himmler had been summarily dismissed from the make-believe Doenitz government located at Flensburg on May 6. Doenitz wanted no Nazi of Himmler's stripe at hand as he attempted to deal with the victorious Allies. Only the day before Himmler's dismissal, the admiral had heard of a typical Himmler-type conference; the SS leader intended to head a new "reformed" Nazi government and treat with the Western powers as an independent state. Doenitz also heard that a *Luftwaffe* squadron, taking Himmler's orders about the Werewolves to heart, was preparing to go underground. He strangled the idiotic but sinister plan at its birth by reminding the members of Himmler's staff that he had forbidden the Werewolves to function. Doenitz knew that they could serve no useful purpose after the unconditional surrender and could complicate relations with the Anglo-American forces.[24]

With no general plan in mind as far as anyone could tell, the former SS *Reichsfuehrer* wandered about the Flensburg area from the time of his dismissal until May 21. On that day he left Flensburg apparently with the idea of going south. It is entirely possible, in view of his complete belief in the *Alpenfestung*, that he may have had the idea of trying to join Kaltenbrunner and Skorzeny somewhere in the area. He became, however, the victim of his own narrow, bureaucratic efficiency. He, like his one-time princeling,

129

Kaltenbrunner, tried to disguise himself by shaving off his mustache. He also affected a patch over his left eye. At a time when most German troops milled about with few if any identifying papers as they passed through Allied control points, Himmler and eleven others in his party carried meticulously prepared false papers. The bogus identification listed Himmler as Heinrich Hitzinger, a member of the Secret Field *Gendarmerie* which, since 1942, had been a part of the infamous Gestapo. Naturally, the Allies had the organization on its list of sinister organizations whose members were to be taken into custody whenever found. Himmler's choice of the Gestapo disguise was, according to one British historian, "a strange indication" of how little, even at that late date, he understood the world revulsion at his activities.[25]

Himmler's journey to the south with the hope of reaching the National Redoubt was destined to end almost at once in the north. His party was picked up by the British at Meinstadt midway between Bremerhaven and Bremen on the day it started. If the group had had no papers in hand, it probably would have been allowed to pass on its way along with ordinary ex-soldiers of the German army. With Gestapo classification, however, they were taken into custody. The British did not realize who Himmler was for almost a full day. Then suddenly, for reasons known only to himself, the former SS leader revealed his identity. He was searched twice, but during the second search on May 23, he bit into a potassium-cyanide pellet hidden in a gum cavity and died within twelve minutes despite desperate efforts to save him.[26]

With Himmler's death and the capture of Goering and Kaltenbrunner the wartime myth of the *Alpen-festung* ended. The actual conquest of the National Redoubt area which American intelligence, Nazi propagandists, and many soldiers of both sides predicted might require months or even years, had been accomplished in something less than three weeks. Confusion over the Redoubt, however, lingered on.

Reprise and

Critique

Part 4

11

There never was a National Redoubt that could have supported effective guerrilla operations or provided a true inner-defensive system by 1944–1945. The populace was disaffected, leadership was lacking, and neither practical operational plans nor supplies existed. It is true that such a fortress complex could have been built if construction had begun in the early war years when time, materials, and manpower were available. If this plan had been implemented, the *Alpenfestung* might have proved a tough reality, deadly to combat, just as its Swiss counterpart was—and is. But, of course, such was the elation over easily won victories and the arrogance of Germany's leadership in the period from 1939 to 1943 that a defensive-fortress concept was unthinkable. Indeed, this was Hitler's position almost to the end. The OKW became interested in the *Alpen-*

festung out of desperation when it was far too late to be of any significant military value. It is a curious irony that the OKW, the American military leaders, and the Russians, each in their own fashion, assessed the feasibility of a National Redoubt in somewhat similar ways.

The German war leaders were so convinced of the inevitable clash between Eastern and Western Allies that they actually believed the Redoubt could be utilized to drive between them a wedge that would be to Germany's advantage. Creaking and straining as the Grand Alliance was, the Nazis ignored the fact that their own conduct was so reprehensible as to force the Allies into a rickety but effective coalition no matter how unnatural. The Russians, ever suspicious, were sure the Redoubt was being used for purposes of a separate peace. United States military leaders, too, were fearful of the Redoubt's being employed as a device to split the alliance. The major mistake of the Americans was in thinking that the German leaders at so late a date had the unity of will and material means to create a National Redoubt.

Even after the evidence was in, the idea persisted in the minds of Eisenhower and Bedell Smith that the shift of American troops to the south had precluded use of the Redoubt as envisioned by Himmler, Hofer, and Kaltenbrunner.

Such a view is only partially correct, because it obscures the true situation. In the Supreme Commander's report to the Combined Chiefs of Staff, compiled in 1945 after the Germans had surrendered, he wrote that preventing a German withdrawal to the Redoubt area "was a major objective in any operations which we might execute in the south." Included in the report were estimates that the bulk of the SS and some 30 armored divisions might "conceivably be concentrated behind mountain barriers." Speed was essential to over-run the area and forestall fortification of the region against attack. The report admitted that although "there was no evidence of any completed system of defenses along the natural ramparts, some progress appeared to have been made in this respect along the northern flank." It went on to say that air reconnaissance revealed underground construction and that "it was believed subterranean factories had been established in the area." Even with the success of Patton's Danube-valley drive, Eisenhower reported that SHAEF thought that "it might still be possible for the Redoubt to hold out."[1]

Eisenhower's report ignores several factors which it might have included had his intelligence been used correctly. His own Rhineland and Ruhr campaigns had been so successful that the bulk of the German army in the west had truly ceased to be an effective force capable of an orderly withdrawal into the Redoubt. It had lost most of its artillery, for one thing, on the west bank of the Rhine. Whatever stiff opposition it was able to offer was local and sporadic. As stated, the OKW lost control of the battle by March and April. The Redoubt never had defenses capable of holding off a determined attack even of lesser size than the one mounted against it. Also, the only defensive positions capable of resisting a sustained attack were in the south and thanks to Karl Wolff, Allen Dulles, and high-level apathy among the SS in Italy, the southern tier of positions were to be surrendered prematurely anyway, no matter what the Americans were doing to the west, north, and east. Without those positions, contrary to Eisenhower's statement about continued resistance, the fortress area was militarily useless.

Furthermore, despite the Supreme Commander's belief that the Redoubt's northern flank showed some signs of a defense system, it was in that area where the German defensive efforts were found to be weakest. With one or two exceptions, the feared underground factories proved to be an illusion. And finally, German civilian morale as well as that of the SS top hierarchy was too badly shaken during the months of March, April, and May to support any resistance within the Redoubt of either an irregular or regular military variety. Without clearheaded leadership, bolstered by a determined civil populace, the *Alpenfestung* never could have been a reality in any case. None of these ingredients expected by Eisenhower, Smith and Bradley were found in paramount form within the National Redoubt. Without them the Redoubt was exactly what nonbelievers said it was—a chimera.

Although the postwar political consequences of Eisenhower's shifting the balance of his attack have aroused great critical comment, in fairness the situation must be seen within the period of the time when it occurred. Since those climactic days, it has been charged that American civil and military leaders were singularly shortsighted in not following Churchill's pleas to drive as far to the east as possible. The assumption is that if the United States had availed itself of the military opportunities presented, it could, in some unexplained fashion, have first forced the Russians into an eastern withdrawal and retreated westward later.

As the economist and diplomatic historian, Herbert Feis and the military historian, Forrest C. Pogue, both have pointed out, however, there was no guarantee that such action would have worked unless the American and British people were willing to maintain large combat-ready armies in position in Eastern and Central Europe for a long period of time. In the spring of 1945 the defeat of Japan was still a prime consideration for both governments. In the United States especially, there was great pressure from the public to bring veteran troops home from Europe, and a military need to redeploy the less seasoned troops in Europe for further duty in the Pacific.[2]

In England, there had long been a critical manpower shortage and thousands of her soldiers were earmarked for return to industrial pursuits. Results of the atomic project were increasingly hopeful, but those few Americans who knew of the weapon wished to await the final test. The new President also wished to try and settle differences through negotiations rather than rely at the outset on armed force. He turned aside Church-

139

ill's adjurations, preferring to wait. Also, at that time, his military advisers still hoped for Russian participation in the Pacific war to reduce expected heavy American casualties, although it is painfully clear in retrospect that Soviet help not only was not needed, but that the Russians would have moved against Japan anyway. They did not need to be bribed or pressured as the American government then imagined.[3]

It may simply have been beyond Eisenhower's responsibility and his experience at that point in his career to have judged the political consequences of his strategy and tactics. Neither he nor his American colleagues had been trained or ordered to operate professionally in such a fashion. The Supreme Commander never received any actual political directives from either the British or American governments or their military staffs regarding Berlin and Prague. The British believed that their influence was weak in the closing days of the European war and the bitterly protracted arguments over Eisenhower's shift from a northern to a central thrust seemed to confirm their beliefs. His decision to seal off the Danish Peninsula and overrun the National Redoubt was based upon what he considered his prime military duty to be.

If guilt is to be assigned for political ingenuousness, it is a collective one shared not only by SHAEF but by the two wartime Presidents and their diplomatic and military advisers, as well. President Truman's responsibility, however, can hardly be equated with his predecessor's. Truman could only follow the advice of men he had to consider more experienced than himself. And he did exactly that.

Eisenhower's concern over the National Redoubt as a military reality may be questioned more seriously. In this case, the American reaction to the *Alpenfestung* was an error in the evaluation of military intelligence. Reduction of the Redoubt offered Eisenhower and Bradley one of several military reasons to stop short of Berlin and Prague and not get involved in an entangling political situation. Why there was such a mistaken evaluation of the available evidence on the mountain citadel and its untoward influence upon SHAEF's strategic and tactical thinking remains the puzzle.

Several reasons why the Redoubt affected Eisenhower's and Bradley's decision have already been discussed: irritation with Montgomery's caution, and a desire to allow the angry and frustrated Bradley to advance adventurously were two of them. The latter factor was stressed in paragraph six of the March 21 "Reorientation of Strategy" directive issued by Twelfth Army Group. Then, too, there was Eisenhower's and Bradley's reluctance to expend any more lives than necessary, and the indication seemed to be that more lives might be lost if the Redoubt was built up. The Supreme Commander also had a moral repugnance toward further destruction and bloodshed, which buttressed his professional assessment of the situation. In addition, American military tradition did not place much stress on warfare as an extension of political policy. Finally, the advice from Washington by Marshall was that in his view quick seizure of the Alpine area was a necessity.[4]

Perhaps there was another consideration somewhat psychological in nature. Military intelligence presented a mixed record in the campaigns of the Western Allies. Among its primary failures were its inability to ascertain how the Norman hedgerow or *bocage* country would be so effectively utilized by the enemy for defensive purposes; the confusion in evaluating the facts of the German build-up prior to the winter Ardennes offensive when the evidence was available; and finally, the undue preoccupation with the alleged danger of the National Redoubt.[5]

A partial explanation for the preoccupation with the Redoubt may lie in the lessons of the first two cases. There may be a hint in a remark Bedell Smith once made in reference to ignoring the defensive potentialities of the Norman *bocage* country. He admitted that the hedgerows should have come as no surprise to the Americans. The French supplied the Americans with information on them and Field Marshal Sir Alan Brooke and other British generals had fought their way out of France in 1940 through the *bocage*. The British were not hopeful about the Americans being able to handle the problem presented by the sunken lanes bounded by the impenetrable brush. There was no lack of accurate detail on the *bocage*, but according to Smith, the Americans refused to believe any of it. The situation seemed beyond their imagination. What was unfamiliar was improbable. "The fact was that we had

142

to get into the country and be bruised by it before we could really take a measure of it," said Smith.[6]

Only a few months later a somewhat analogous situation developed with respect to the Ardennes winter battle. Both British and American intelligence failed to read the implications of the facts at hand. While acknowledging that a small spoiling attack might come, none of the top commanders believed that the Germans would mount a full-scale offensive because it seemed obviously militarily unsound. As a result, the Allies, especially the Americans, were bruised in brutal fashion by the scope and intensity of the abortive German attack which was carried out at Hitler's irrational order.[7]

Conceivably, by the time reports on the Redoubt began to filter into intelligence sections, there was a subconscious or maybe even a conscious effort to rectify the previous errors. Eisenhower, Bradley, and Smith all have stated that the evidence of the Redoubt was too strong to ignore—and in view of their past sad experience in intelligence evaluation, perhaps it was decidedly too ominous to brush aside.

Much of the so-called evidence was fallacious, but there may have been a compulsion to believe it. Eisenhower, however, flatly rejects this theory, stating that his staff was made up "of competent, experienced men" and not "a group of people that gives way to hysterical emotion." With reference to the Ardennes, he has stated that the mistaken estimates concerning the Battle of the Bulge "were not particularly erroneous." Eisenhower says he knew of the build-up, but that he and Bradley were wrong in figuring out the Germans' "timing," thus allowing them "a very considerable penetration." According to the Supreme Commander, neither he nor his headquarters was sensitive because of the criticism over the intelligence work connected with the Ardennes. They were, says the former Supreme Commander, too busy after the Bulge to read any deprecating charges.

He believes that adverse comments about intelligence during the winter battle did not condition their reaction to the Redoubt. In Eisenhower's own words, ". . . it seems unlikely that we could have been consciously or unconsciously influenced in our later thinking by this kind of error in our G-2 estimates. . . ." Possibly the former Supreme Commander is entirely right, but there remains the fact that he and his colleagues did overestimate the Redoubt and the earlier intelligence failures definitely could have been one of the unacknowledged reasons the Americans decided to take no chances on the *Alpenfestung*. They were not going to allow it to develop to the point where it, too, could bruise them before they could take a measure of it.[8]

The misreading of intelligence concerning the National Redoubt is ironic in many respects, not the least of which is that no World War II commander had a greater concern about intelligence evaluation than Eisenhower. He has explained in writing and others have also noted that the United States Army's Intelligence service was in a deplorable state as we entered the war. As is well known now, G-2 was the Army's stepchild, starved for funds, and staffed too often by amateurs and incompetents if fully staffed at all. In Africa, Eisenhower got badly burned by faulty intelligence work in connection with the German attack at Kasserine Pass during the early winter of 1943. From that experience he learned to demand (and get) competent intelligence staff officers. In selecting personnel for his G-2 section at SHAEF, he tried to pick the men he considered to be the very best.

It was felt by a number of Americans that much could be learned from the British in such work and Eisenhower himself was especially impressed by one particular British intelligence officer. The man was Major General Kenneth W. D. Strong, whom the Supreme Commander had selected as his G-2 at Allied Forces Headquarters in the Mediterranean theater after the Kasserine Pass defeat. Strong was an acknowledged expert of long standing in the field of German affairs. When Eisenhower moved to England to plan the continental invasion, he insisted that Strong be reassigned to SHAEF.[9]

Strong's appointment was hard to obtain, for his superb qualities made him a prize on any staff. Finally, on May 25, 1944, only thirteen days before D-Day, he took over as G-2 at Eisenhower's headquarters. Strong generally organized the SHAEF G-2 section along British lines. His chief deputy was an American, Brigadier Thomas J. Betts, who had served on the Washington War Department G-2 and another deputy was Brigadier E. J. Foord of the British army, also a man of experience. SHAEF's G-2 did not directly collect information. It depended upon subordinate units to do this and forward the material to the highest headquarters. So SHAEF received data and estimates from its army groups, from the OSS, from the War and Navy Departments, the British Joint Intelligence Committee in London, and from Resistance organizations behind the German defenses.[10]

Criticisms, however, may be made of certain practices under Strong's stewardship at SHAEF. They were not his fault but were caused by the working conditions in an allied staff section.* The glue of an alliance—compromise—is also its curse. In order to administer his section without friction and with as much efficiency as possible, Strong had to adopt certain American practices. After all, the Supreme Commander and his Chief of Staff were both Americans. Strong, laboring under such handicaps, may too often have been forced to adopt some bad procedure used by many United States Army staffs. Unlike an all-British G-2 section, the Americans would present to a commander all the possible alternatives of action the enemy might choose, without necessarily stressing the likeliest. This meant that the commander was not given

* A former American member of SHAEF informed the author that in his opinion Strong was sometimes too self-effacing when dealing with Smith. The result, said the informant (who may not be identified), was that Smith may have mistaken Strong's reticence on certain questions as some form of acquiescence when such was not always the case.

a clear lead and too often had to select from a smör-gåsbord of information. If a bad line of reasoning was followed, as in the cases of Ardennes or the Redoubt, G-2 was able to say in defense that its basis was only one of many considerations offered the commander. G-2 had done its job in evaluating and presenting as much material as possible for selection. The British, by contrast, had evolved during World War II a different type of intelligence evaluation. Their technique was to inform a commander of the enemy's most likely course of action and his capabilities to achieve it.[11]

In using an all-British technique, alternatives were discussed, of course, but through experience any protectively obscure language was eliminated. This procedure was not always possible in a supreme headquarters composed of personnel from two nations and working from different sets of practices. The very rarefied nature of SHAEF, also, precluded Strong's seeing the evidence at first hand. Of necessity, it was served up to him. Finally, Strong, in a subordinate position, had to give Eisenhower or Smith the type of information they thought they needed to assess situations. There were severe limitations imposed on Strong's great skills by the very nature of the Allied headquarters to which he was assigned. In short, his talents may not have been utilized as wisely as they might have been.[12]

The British had also learned to rely upon a tremendous number of civilians who eventually held senior appointments in their military intelligence.

Many were academicians and their attitude was that of scholars in uniform even though the majority were required to have extensive combat-duty experience before assuming staff duties. These men, well-versed experts, trained to analyze odd bits of information, knew what intelligence was to be used for and they were the ones who briefed their commanders. Under the American procedure, not only was there a plethora of material from which to make difficult choices, but the people who really understood the information were not necessarily those who briefed the commanders.

In World War II many American Regular Army personnel, lacking the necessary experience or training, held senior G-2 positions. Good as some of these men were, too many were little more than technicians and practically none of the men in top positions were experts in the British sense. Thus, American commanders were often forced to operate in a confused atmosphere.[13]

Strong added one feature to the SHAEF intelligence section that met with only lukewarm approval by General Walter Bedell Smith—a Joint Intelligence Committee, which was to keep under constant surveillance military and political affairs for which Eisenhower was responsible. In the words of SHAEF's official historian, "It was to be the sole producer of intelligence appreciations for the Planning Staff, SHAEF, and be the final authority on all intelligence matters for SHAEF." The Chief of Staff's objection to the new arrangement was that it sanctioned a committee-type command system which Eisenhower disliked and wished to avoid.[14]

Nonetheless, Strong prevailed and all the information collected at SHAEF was evaluated and then passed downward in weekly intelligence summaries.* Naturally, there was a time lag before the material was disseminated and also, to protect sources, certain items were omitted from the summaries. In practice, the Supreme Commander and the army group commanders came to rely on personal briefings by their intelligence chiefs or staff members for the latest and most accurate assessments. Relations between the SHAEF G-2 intelligence personnel and the subordinate army groups were described as "cordial" by SHAEF's historian, Forrest C. Pogue. But, again, according to Pogue, the same harmony did not exist between the army groups and the armies serving under their direction and the army groups depended primarily on the lower echelons for their basic information.[15]

As the vast intelligence systems for the Allied Armies are scrutinized, it may be seen where it was possible for errors of omission and commission to occur. One of the oddities about the Redoubt myth was that by the very end of March and the beginning of April SHAEF's G-2 was increasingly skeptical of the National Redoubt's strength. By contrast, Seventh Army,

* The *After Action Reports* of the Twelfth Army were very complimentary to the weekly intelligence summaries.

under Devers' Sixth Army Group, swallowed the story whole, while as late as April 24 Bradley, commanding the Twelfth Army Group was terribly depressed about the Redoubt's potential. Another striking aspect of all intelligence concerning the *Alpenfestung* was that there was no unanimity among various sections about what it truly represented.

As already observed, the OSS both in Europe and in Washington downgraded the fortress theory, but there is no available evidence that they officially passed their misgivings on to G-2 or that, if the Army Intelligence experts did receive such information, they believed it. Relations between the armies and their OSS sections varied from army to army. General Courtney H. Hodges' First Army G-2 ruled the OSS out of his domain during the winter of 1944–1945, but Patton's Third Army G-2 praised its versatility and value.[16] G-2 in Washington apparently was divided on the subject of the Redoubt; Marshall veered toward its believers; SHAEF's G-2 was also split.

Initially, in February, many members ignored the reports on the *Alpenfestung* and then changed and tended to believe the information in March and early April. Generally, SHAEF's G-2 personnel appear to have altered their evaluations rather more quickly than the Twelfth Army Group's G-2 and the G-2 of the Seventh Army despite the fact that the two subordinate organizations were closer to the scene. There was never any absolute unanimity of opinion, however, about the Redoubt's alleged purposes on any level anywhere within the Western Allied Armies. SHAEF finally decided it would be a bastion from which guerrillas could operate and this view in time was the one adopted by most lower echelons. Save in the Seventh Army where the fortress idea tended to persist! But in such large structures as SHAEF and its armies, time lags in disseminating the intelligence evaluations, lack of harmony between upper and lower headquarters, and inflexible lines of authority and responsibility may also have helped to account for the confusion about the Redoubt. The Twelfth Army Group's *After Operations Report* stated that its Army G-2 sections too often were understaffed and that its liaison officers were poorly trained. The critique also noted that lateral dissemination of data between the armies and their corps was slow.[17]

SHAEF, for example, knew of Wolff's surrender maneuvers and was interested because they indicated a weakening of German determination, but Italy was outside of its area of responsibility. The fact that a capitulation in Italy would rip the heart out of the Redoubt and make it lifeless does not, however, seem to have been acknowledged by Eisenhower.

Dissemination is an extremely weak area of intelligence work. Standard bureaucratic procedure may see documents of importance processed in such a fashion that key personnel never receive the information at all or else receive it too late. Actually, in the Redoubt's case, SHAEF's appreciations in several respects appear to have been more realistic than those of many of its subordinate units, save for the British Twenty-first Army Group. But its comprehensive appreciations

151

during April apparently did not greatly impress Bradley.

Failure to evaluate the credibility of the Redoubt stories did not have a disastrous effect upon the progress of American arms in the European theater. However, the American preoccupation with the *Alpenfestung* may lend some ammunition to critics of our World War II civil and military naïveté in the use of conventional war as a means of obtaining political ends.

The myth of the National Redoubt, it would seem, illustrates some traditional pitfalls within the American military intelligence services. A mere accumulation of material does not add up to any real knowledge. Too much accumulation makes extremely difficult the pertinent selection of what is considered valuable. There was, thanks to the Germans, a plethora of half-truths about the Redoubt and during April some hard evidence concerning it. But the actual fact was that there was no fortress or group of leaders capable of organizing a guerrilla movement. Intelligence officers failed completely to ascertain how materially and morally bankrupt the Nazi leadership was in the last three months of the war. As British intelligence officers realized, the very personalities supposed to be the creators and leaders of the *Alpenfestung* and German resistance movements were psychologically and mentally incapable of getting the job done.

Conditioned by all of the factors previously discussed, many American leaders and intelligence officers

152

seem to have settled upon an oversimplified obsession with an easily recognized military situation. Based on their experiences, it seemed probable the Nazis could and would try some type of operation within the Alps. Having decided this, there may have been a concerted effort by various intelligence staffs on all levels to collect the evidence to prove that their hypothesis was the correct one and that it could be confirmed by troop withdrawals, the evacuation of government officials from Berlin, rhetorical speeches about last-ditch defenses, and sinister references to the Werewolves. Ham-handed, unimaginative German attempts to split the East and West over the Redoubt problem supported those who contended the last stand would be made there.

To the very pragmatic Americans, trying extremely hard to end combat operations in the shortest possible time, it seemed logically illogical of the Nazis to try to create an *Alpenfestung*. However stupid and bloody such a course might be, Americans dwelt upon it while in truth it was not at all a likely risk at that point in the war's finale. Having set the course of the strategy, Eisenhower, in effect, forced the German army into the National Redoubt, which further seemed to verify the thesis. As we know, a bare few on the German side wanted to use the *Alpenfestung* for fighting. Most sought it as an asylum.

One American intelligence expert, formerly of the OSS, has candidly expressed the view that moments of greatest success among intelligence officers are the very instances "which produce the greatest goosiness among G-2's." They simply "cannot allow themselves to believe that the good news is not full of worms." Their advice, as a result, is often unimaginative and paradoxically, dangerously cautious.[18]

With the National Redoubt in mind, it could be said that because of such intelligence practices, the military leaders formulated a plan that was basically unsophisticated and made little allowance for diversity.

This is not to say that the area should not have been overrun. But it is to suggest that it might have been reduced with far less force, thus allowing Eisenhower more troops to deploy elsewhere. He felt that he could and would have taken Berlin if it could have been done "cheaply." He might have been able to do just that by buttressing his central and northern armies with some of those many units he had needlessly sent south into the Redoubt. If the Western Allies had gone to Berlin, it is true that they would eventually have had to withdraw, save for the token forces within their occupation sectors of the city. But it is also just possible that if the Americans and British had marched into the German capital and confronted the Russians, the Western powers might have realized far earlier than they did that they should not withdraw until the vexatious question of Allied access rights to the city had been settled. Twenty-twenty hindsight is a luxury historians possess; it is also their responsibility to study the origins of the Berlin problem.

Conceivably, having taken the plunge toward Berlin, Eisenhower may also have found it possible to have moved on to Prague. By May 4, he realized he was able to do this, owing to the unexpected collapse of the Redoubt. Washington was not completely immune to the idea. What was needed was a bolder, more imaginative appreciation of the political and military situation by both Washington and SHAEF. Washington, over British protests, insisted that the initiative be given to the Supreme Commander, allowing him to decide. He, of course, passed the responsibility right back to Washington and the Combined Chiefs. No clear and decisive political lead was given Eisenhower and with victory within his grasp, he acted cautiously.

The Redoubt's reduction was, in many respects, a wasted strategic and tactical operation. The lessons of why this was so are valid for study now. Briefly and theoretically, what should have happened is as follows: the political consequences of both strategic and tactical military operations should have been considered and evaluated on the basis of a scholarly analysis as much as upon what was militarily expeditious. The strategic and tactical intelligence involved was too empirical and should have been slightly more metempirical. What seemed likely from the logical American point of view turned out to be an unreality. Intelligence personnel should have realized that what seemed illogical often proved to be very probable, and top commanders should have been presented with a far more sophisticated appreciation of the enemy's most likely course of action and his capabilities to undertake it.

There was a poverty of penetrating insight among too many of the intelligence personnel and the top commanders. They took too much at face value because, on the basis of their past experiences, it seemed to fit their preconceived views of what should happen. Because the SS had fought savagely during the winter and the early spring and because its leaders had a reputation for fanaticism, it seemed logical that the elite corps of troops would hold out in the Redoubt. But, as we have seen, the top leadership was disintegrating steadily from the late winter weeks on, and Wolff's dealings with Dulles should have been but one significant example of this. As pointed out earlier, the tip was not heeded. Allowance should have been made for the almost total decay of German leadership; instead, courses of action were adopted that fitted a familiar, simple-minded plan. These mistakes born of reductionism are only too easy for intelligence officers and commanders to repeat.

Intelligence evaluations of all types from the tactical up to the national level are incredibly important for our defense in this age. Highly trained researchers are needed on all levels of intelligence work. It is conceivable that if more such people had been employed in tactical as well as strategic intelligence activities, and if the results of their work had been properly disseminated in 1945, the Redoubt affair might have been seen in its proper perspective.

In the relief of 1945's victory, the United States obscured the lessons of the Redoubt. In a limited sense it could afford to. After all, the Allies had won overwhelmingly and the exposure of the National Redoubt's myth seemed but a small mistake measured against the magnitude of victory.

But the lessons are important on two counts. A different evaluation and a proper dissemination of information in both Washington and SHAEF might have altered history in Central and Eastern Europe, and in the light of this possibility, it is well to remember that today there are no longer such things as "minor" intelligence errors. They add up to an insupportable weight. Perhaps this knowledge is the *Alpenfestung's* legacy. If so, it may well be the best aspect of its peculiar history.

Notes

INTRODUCTION

[1] For an explanation of the Allied strategy, see Dwight D. Eisenhower, *Crusade in Europe* (Dolphin Paperback Co., New York, 1960), pp. 240–242. For the decision to aim toward Berlin, see *SHAEF Planning Draft of Post-Neptune Courses of Action After the Capture of the Lodgment Area, Main Objectives and the Axes of Advance*, I, 3 May 1944, SHAEF SGS Post Overlord Planning, 381, I. The source is the Secretary of the General Staff, SHAEF, files and was cited in Kent Greenfield (ed.), *Command Decisions* (Harcourt, Brace and Co., New York, 1959), pp. 377, 458.

[2] Forrest C. Pogue, *The Supreme Command; the European Theater of Operations; United States Army in World War II Series* (Office of the Chief of Military History, Department of the Army, Washington, D.C., 1954), p. 434. (Hereafter referred to as Pogue, *The Supreme Command*.)

[3] *Ibid.*

[4] *Report by the Supreme Commander to the Combined Chiefs of Staff on the Operations in Europe of the Allied Expeditionary Force, 6 June 1944 to 8 May 1945* (Government Printing Office, Washington, D.C., 1945), pp. 105–106, 112–116. (Hereafter referred to as Eisenhower, *Report by the Supreme Commander*.)

[5] Omar N. Bradley, *A Soldier's Story* (Holt, Rinehart and Winston, Inc., New York, 1951), p. 536.

CHAPTER 1

[1] George S. Patton, Jr., annotated by Colonel Paul D. Harkins, *War as I Knew It* (Houghton Mifflin, Boston, 1947), pp. 308–317; also, Fred Clinger, Arthur Johnston, and Vincent Masel, *The History of the Seventy-first Infantry Division* (Augsburg, 1947) (hereafter cited as Clinger, *et al.*, *The History of the Seventy-first Infantry Division*); Robert S. Allen, *Lucky Forward: The Story of Patton's Third U.S. Army* (Vanguard Press, New York, 1947), p. 383; William East and William Gleason, *The 409th Infantry in World War II* (Infantry Journal Press, Washington, 1947), pp. 136–145; Trezzvant W. Anderson, *Come Out Fighting: The Epic Tale of the 761st Battalion, 1942–1945* (Salzburg, 1945), p. 89; Kenneth Kozen, *The Fourth Armored Division from the Beach to Bavaria—The Story of the Fourth Armored Division in Combat* (Munich, 1946), p. 145; Ralph E. Pearson, *Enroute to the Redoubt: A Soldier's Report as a Regiment Goes to War* (Adams Printing Service, Chicago, Illinois, 1957), III, 178–201 (hereafter cited as Pearson, *Enroute to the Redoubt*); Melvin J. Lasky, *Seventh Army—Field Notes on the Disintegration of the German Army* (Augsburg, 1945), unpublished MS, Office of the Chief of Military History (OCMH files), pp. 4–20 (hereafter referred to as Lasky, *Field Notes*, OCMH files).

160

² John P. Delaney, *The Blue Devils in Italy—A History of the 88th Infantry Division in World War II* (Infantry Journal Press, Washington, 1947), pp. 218–219; Chester G. Starr (ed.), *From Salerno to the Alps: A History of the Fifth Army, 1943–1945* (Infantry Journal Press, Washington, 1948), pp. 432–437. Lucien K. Truscott, Jr., *Command Decisions: A Personal History* (E. P. Dutton, New York, 1954), pp. 476–504.

³ Delaney, *The Blue Devils*, pp. 218–220.

⁴ *Ibid.*, pp. 218–231.

CHAPTER 2

¹ *Trial of the Major War Criminals Before the International Military Tribunal* (Nuremberg, 1948), XXI, 9 (hereafter cited as *I.M.T.*). The projected invasion was code named *Jolka* or "Christmas Tree." See also, Jon Kimche, *Spying for Peace: General Guisan and Swiss Neutrality* (Weidenfeld and Nicolson, London, 1962), p. 52 (hereafter referred to as Kimche, *Spying for Peace*).

² *Generalmajor* Marcinkiewicz, *Report on the Alpenfestung* (Allendorf, June, 1946, MS No. B-187, OCMH files), pp. 2–4 (hereafter cited as Marcinkiewicz, *Report*); *General der Pionier* Alfred Jacob, *Report Concerning the German Alpine Redoubt* (Allendorf, 1946, MS No. B-188, OCMH files), pp. 1–2 (hereafter cited as Jacob, *Report on the Alpine Redoubt*); *General der Gebirgstruppen* Georg Ritter von Hengl, *Report on the Alpine Fortress* (April, 1946, MS No. B-459, OCMH files), pp. 4–6 (hereafter referred as to Von Hengl, *Report on the Fortress*).

³ War Department, Military Intelligence Division, *German Mountain Warfare*, Special Series, No. 21 (Government Printing Office, Washington, 1944).

⁴ Willi Frischauer, *The Rise and Fall of Hermann Goering* (Houghton Mifflin, Boston, 1951), p. 244.

[5] Rudolf Aschenauer, *Der Fall Schoerner; Eine Klarstellung* (Privately Printed, Munich, 1962), p. 8 (hereafter referred to as Aschenauer, *Der Fall Schoerner*); Wilhelm Hoettl, *Hitler's Paper Weapon* (R. Hart and Davis, London, 1945), p. 148.

[6] Forrest C. Pogue, *The Supreme Command*, pp. 171–230, 244–260, 279–318; Vincent J. Esposito Jr., ed., *The West Point Atlas of American Wars* (Praeger, New York, 1959), II, Map 99 (hereafter referred to as Esposito, *West Point Atlas*).

[7] Marcinkiewicz, *Report*, pp. 1–2.

[8] *Ibid.*, pp. 3–5.

[9] United States Office of Strategic Services, Research and Analysis Branch, R and A No. 232, *South Germany: An Analysis of the Political and Social Organization, the Communications, Economic Controls, Agriculture and Food Supply, Mineral Resources, Manufacturing and Transportation Facilities of South Germany* (Washington, 1944) (hereafter referred to as OSS Report No. 232, *South Germany*).

[10] Franz Hofer, *Alpenstellung—Alpenfestung* (MS No. 457 and Annex No. 1, OCMH files), Annex No. 1, pp. 1–2 (hereafter referred to as Hofer, *Alpenstellung*, Annex Nos. 1, 2, 3).

[11] For books dealing with the Nazis and Hitler, see Alan L. C. Bullock, *Hitler: A Study in Tyranny* (Harper and Row, rev. ed., New York, 1962); Gerald Reitlinger, *The SS, Alibi of a Nation, 1922–1945* (Heineman, London, 1956), and Hugh R. Trevor-Roper, *The Last Days of Hitler* (Macmillan New York, 1947).

[12] Ladestas Farago, *Burn After Reading: The Espionage of World War II* (Walker and Co., New York, 1961), pp. 269–271, (hereafter referred to as Farago, *Burn After Reading*); Hofer, *Alpenstellung*, Annex No. 1, p. 2; Kimche, *op. cit.*, pp. 126–154; Hoettl, *Hitler's Paper Weapon*, pp. 147–148.

[13] Hofer, *Alpenstellung*, Annex No. 1, pp. 3–5.

[14] *Ibid.;* OSS Report No. 232, *South Germany*, pp. 1–129; Marcinkiewicz, *Report*, pp. 13–14.

[15] Hofer, *Alpenstellung*, Annex No. 1, pp. 3–5.

[16] *Ibid.*, Annex No. 3, pp. 1–2.

[17] *Ibid.*, pp. 2–6. It was Hofer who named the Redoubt the *Alpenfestung*, the term which the Germans came to employ.

[18] *Ibid.*, pp. 6–9.

[19] Marcinkiewicz, *Report*, pp. 5–12.

[20] Harry Vosser, "Hitler's Hideaway," The New York *Times* magazine section, Nov. 12, 1944, p. 36; Reitlinger, *op. cit.*, pp. 249–250.

[21] Walter Hagen (pseud.), *Unternehmen Bernhard; ein historischer Tatsachenbericht—uber die grosste Geldfalschungsaktion aller Zeiten* (Welsund Stornberg, Verlag Welsermühl, 1955), pp. 231–232 (hereafter referred to as Hagen, *Unternehmen Bernhard*); Pogue, *The Supreme Command*, pp. 359–361; *The Daily Worker* (New York), Dec. 15, 1944, 12:3–5; Aschenauer, *Der Fall Schoerner*, p. 88.

[22] Hagen, *Unternehmen Bernhard*, p. 231.

[23] *Ibid.*, pp. 231–232.

[24] *Ibid.*, also, Hoettl, *Hitler's Paper Weapon*, pp. 148–149; also, Wilhelm Hoettl, as told to Ladislas Farago, "I Was Hitler's Master Spy," *Argosy*, CCCXXXVII (November, 1953), p. 81.

[25] *Ibid.*

[26] Hofer, *Alpenstellung*, Annex No. 3, pp. 2–9; Aschenauer, *op. cit.*, p. 87; Pogue, *The Supreme Command*, pp. 398–404; Kimche, *op. cit.*, pp. 119–125, 126–154; Hagen, *Unternehmen Bernhard*, pp. 231–233.

[27] Marcinkiewicz, *Report*, pp. 7–11; Milton Shulman, *Defeat in the West* (E. P. Dutton, New York, 1948), p. 291; Bradley, *Soldier's Story*, pp. 536–537.

[28] *The Daily Worker* (New York), Dec. 24, 1944,

12:3–5; *The Daily Worker* (New York), Jan. 26, 1945, 12:3–5; Erwin Lessner, "Hitler's Final V Weapon," *Collier's* magazine, Jan. 27, 1945, p. 14.

[29] Reitlinger, *op. cit.*, pp. 382, 445–446; Pogue, *op. cit.*, pp. 476, 483; Trevor-Roper, *The Last Days*, pp. 44–48.

[30] The New York *Times*, Feb. 1, 1945, 4:4; Reuben E. Jenkins, "The Battle of the German National Redoubt —Planning Phase," *Military Review*, XXVI (1946), 3–8. This account remains one of the best military studies of the National Redoubt. Also, Hoettl, *loc. cit.*, p. 81; Farago, *Burn After Reading*, pp. 271–272.

CHAPTER 3

[1] Farago, *Burn After Reading*, pp. 271–272; Herbert Feis, *Churchill, Roosevelt, Stalin; The War They Waged and the Peace They Sought* (Princeton University Press, Princeton, N.J., 1957), pp. 583–585 (hereafter referred to as Feis, *Churchill, Roosevelt, Stalin*); Kimche, *op. cit.*, pp. 126–154.

[2] *Ibid.*; all the sources cited immediately above are relevant.

[3] *Ibid.*

[4] *Ibid.*; Hofer, *Alpenstellung*, Annex No. 3, pp. 3–9; Aschenauer, *Der Fall Schoerner*, pp. 82–89; Reitlinger, *op. cit.*, pp. 419–420.

[5] Kimche, *op. cit.*, pp. 126–154.

[6] *Ibid.*

[7] The New York *Times*, Feb. 3, 1945, 1:7; Reitlinger, *The SS, Alibi of a Nation*, p. 268; Curt Reiss, *Joseph Goebbels, A Biography* (Doubleday, Garden City, N.Y., 1948), pp. 306–307, 318–320; Rudolf Semmler, *Goebbels, The Man Next to Hitler* (Westhouse, London, 1947), pp. 185–187 (hereafter cited as Semmler, *The Man Next to Hitler*); Roger Manvell and Heinrich Fraenkel, *Doctor Goebbels; His Life and Death* (Heineman, London, 1960),

pp. 260–261 (hereafter referred to as Manvell and Fraenkel, *Doctor Goebbels*).

[8] Reitlinger, *op. cit.*, pp. 268, 419–421; The New York *Times*, Feb. 3, 1945, 1:7. The dispatch was from SHAEF. Also, Aschenauer, *Der Fall Schoerner*, p. 87. For accounts of the rumors circulating in one of America's most responsible newspapers, see The New York *Times*, Feb. 11, 1945, Sec. E–8:1, Victor Schiff, "The Last Fortress of the Nazis: In the East of Switzerland Hitler's Henchmen Are Expected to Make a Final Stand"; The New York *Times*, Feb. 14, 1945, 9:1. The latter dispatch was based upon a monitored radio broadcast from Berlin quoting Dr. Paul Schmidt of the Foreign Service, who threatened that millions of Germans would wage guerrilla warfare and kill ten Allied soldiers for every German who died.

[9] Hanson W. Baldwin, "The War's Course May Hinge on the 'Battle of Berlin'," The New York *Times*, Feb. 4, 1945, Sec. E–5:2; *ibid.*, Feb. 15, 1945, 4:1; *ibid.*, Feb. 5, 1945, 11:1.

[10] Schiff *loc. cit.*, p. 8; Lessner, *loc. cit.*, p. 14; Vosser, *loc. cit.*, p. 36; Hoettl, *loc. cit.*, p. 81; Reitlinger, *op. cit.*, pp. 381–413; Heinz Guderian, *Erinnerungen eines Soldaten* (K. Vowinekel, Heidelberg, 1951), pp. 366–388.

[11] Semmler, *Goebbels, The Man Next to Hitler*, p. 187; Reiss, *Joseph Goebbels, A Biography*, pp. 306–307, 318–322; Pogue, *op. cit.*, pp. 423–424; Bradley, *A Soldier's Story*, pp. 510–513.

[12] The New York *Times*, Mar. 18, 1945, 5:3–6; *The Daily Worker* (New York), Mar. 3, 1945, 12:3–5; *ibid.*, Mar. 13, 1945, 12:3–5; Feis, *Churchill, Roosevelt, Stalin*, pp. 583–596; Farago, *Burn After Reading*, pp. 272–274.

[13] Feis, *op. cit.*, pp. 583–596.

[14] *Ibid.*, Reitlinger, *op. cit.*, pp. 419–420.

[15] Reitlinger, *op. cit.*, pp. 419–421; Farago, *Burn After Reading*, pp. 273–274.

[16] *I.M.T.*, IX, 194; Reitlinger, *op. cit.*, pp. 419–421;

Feis, *op. cit.*, pp. 583–596; Hoettl, *Hitler's Paper Weapon*, pp. 150–156.

CHAPTER 4

[1] *SHAEF Weekly Intelligence Summary No. 51,* 11 Mar. 1945, SHAEF G-2 file, referred to in Pogue, *The Supreme Command,* p. 435; also, Chester Wilmot, *The Struggle for Europe* (Collins, London, 1952), p. 690. Here the pertinent paragraphs of *Summary No. 51* are quoted.

[2] Dwight D. Eisenhower, *Crusade in Europe,* pp. 388–419; Eisenhower, *Report by the Supreme Commander,* pp. 103–105; Pogue, *op. cit.,* pp. 407–440; see Mark Clark, *Calculated Risk* (Harper & Bros., New York, 1950), pp. 348–351; also, Truscott, *Command Decisions,* p. 553; Esposito, *The West Point Atlas, II,* Maps with text, Nos. 66, 67, 68.

[3] Most of these accusations are British. See Chester Wilmot, *The Struggle for Europe,* pp. 690–698, 715 (hereafter cited as Wilmot, *Struggle for Europe*); John Ehrman, *Grand Strategy* (H. M. Stationery Office, London, 1956), VI, 131–163; Milton Shulman, *Defeat in the West,* pp. 277–294; J. F. C. Fuller, *The Second World War, 1939–1945: A Strategical and Tactical History* (Duell, Sloan & Pearce, New York, 1949), p. 361 (hereafter cited as Fuller, *The Second World War*). Also, Arthur Bryant, *Triumph in the West, 1943–1946: Based on the Diaries and Autobiographical Notes of Field Marshal The Viscount Alanbrooke, K.G., O.M.* (Collins, London, 1959), pp. 425–459, 466–482 (hereafter cited as Bryant, *Triumph in the West*). Also, Winston Churchill, *The Second World War: Triumph and Tragedy* (Bantam Paperback Books, New York, 1962), VI, 391–400, 432, 441, 443 (hereafter cited as Churchill, *Triumph and Tragedy*).

[4] Eisenhower, *Crusade in Europe,* pp. 419–427; Brad-

ley, *A Soldier's Story*, pp. 510–546; Walter Bedell Smith, *Eisenhower's Six Great Decisions* (Longmans, Green, New York, 1956), pp. 175–178, 186–201.

[5] *Ibid.*, also, Pogue, *op. cit.*, p. 350; Eisenhower, *Crusade in Europe*, p. 420; Smith, *Eisenhower's Six Great Decisions*, p. 186.

[6] Headquarters Twelfth Army Group, *Reorientation of Strategy*, 21 March 1945, Appendix A, *G-2 Report on German Plans for Continued Resistance, The National Redoubt* (OCMH files) (hereafter referred to as Twelfth Army Group, *Reorientation of Strategy*, with Appendix A, *The National Redoubt*).

[7] *Ibid.*

[8] *Ibid.*, for irritation and criticism over Montgomery's slowness and an American desire to exploit a spectacular, quick offensive, see Bradley, *op. cit.*, pp. 424–425, 511–522; Pogue, *op. cit.*, p. 435; Kent Roberts Greenfield, ed., *Command Decisions*, p. 382.

[9] Twelfth Army Group, *Reorientation of Strategy*, with Appendix A, *The National Redoubt*.

[10] *Ibid.*; also, Twelfth Army Group, *Report of Operations, Final After Action Reports.* (Printed in Europe, 1945, III, 62 hereafter referred to as Twelfth Army Group, *Report of Operations*).

[11] Seventh Army, *Study, German National Redoubt and Related Documents*, 25 March 1945 (OCMH files, No. 107-2.0 hereafter referred to as Seventh Army, *German National Redoubt*).

[12] *Ibid.*

[13] Reitlinger, *The SS, Alibi of a Nation*, pp. 250, 403, 408–413.

[14] *Ibid.*, pp. 414–419.

[15] *Ibid.*, pp. 419–421; Hoettl, *Hitler's Paper Weapon*, pp. 148–151.

[16] Reitlinger, *op. cit.*, p. 421; Hoettl, *Hitler's Paper Weapon*, pp. 151–152.

167

[17] Hoettl, *Hitler's Paper Weapon*, pp. 151–152.
[18] *Ibid.*, pp. 153–155.

CHAPTER 5

[1] Reuben E. Jenkins, "The Battle of the German National Redoubt—Planning Phase," *Military Review*, XXVI (1946), 6; The New York *Times*, Mar. 24, 1945, 5:8, 16:1; The New York *Times*, Mar. 25, 1945, E–1:3–4; *The Daily Worker* (New York), Mar. 14, 1945, 12:3–5; *The Daily Worker* (New York), Mar. 24, 1945, 12:3–5; Pogue, *op. cit.*, p. 436.

[2] Eisenhower, *Crusade in Europe*, pp. 419–427; Bradley, *op. cit.*, pp. 535–537; Pogue, *op. cit.*, pp. 436–437.

[3] Ehrman, *Grand Strategy*, VI, 131–133; Bryant, *Triumph in the West*, pp. 440–442; Bernard L. Montgomery, *The Memoirs of Field Marshal The Viscount Montgomery of Alamein, K. G.* (World Publishing Co., New York and Cleveland, 1958), pp. 296–297 (hereafter referred to as Montgomery, *Memoirs*). Churchill, *Triumph and Tragedy*, pp. 458–460; Shulman, *Defeat in the West*, pp. 286–294; Wilmot, *The Struggle for Europe*, pp. 689–693; Fuller, *The Second World War*, pp. 360–361.

[4] Eisenhower, *Crusade in Europe*, pp. 419–427; Ehrman, *op. cit.*, pp. 131–134; Pogue, *op. cit.*, pp. 436, 441–447; letter from a British intelligence expert, who must remain anonymous, to the author, May 3, 1962.

[5] Based on Letter to the author from Montgomery, June 23, 1963.

[6] Pogue, *op. cit.*, pp. 378–390, 407–416, 434–436; Churchill, *op. cit.*, pp. 395–401; Bryant, *op. cit.*, pp. 441–448; Bradley, *Soldier's Story*, pp. 475–478, 510–521.

[7] Ehrman, *op. cit.*, pp. 133–135; Churchill, *op. cit.*, pp. 390–402; Bryant, *op. cit.*, p. 445.

CHAPTER 6

[1] Churchill, *op. cit.*, pp. 391, 395, 397–402, 416–430; Pogue, *op. cit.*, pp. 441–447; Bryant, *op. cit.*, pp. 441–442; Ehrman, *op. cit.*, pp. 135–136; Feis, *Churchill, Roosevelt, Stalin*, pp. 571–580, 600–612.

[2] Bradley, *op. cit.*, pp. 528, 532–536; Eisenhower, *Crusade in Europe*, pp. 391–394, 419–427; Smith, *Eisenhower's Six Great Decisions*, pp. 186–201; for expressions of United States wartime military policy somewhat devoid of sophisticated ideological or political nuances and considerations, see Ernest R. May, ed., *The Ultimate Decision: The President as Commander in Chief* (G. Braziller, New York, 1960); Pogue, *op. cit.*, pp. 468–469; analysis and the historical evolutions of American military policies and traditions are found in T. Harry Williams, *Americans at War: The Development of the American Military System* (Louisiana State University Press, Baton Rouge, 1960), pp. 3–7, 85–126, and Russell F. Weigley, *Towards an American Army: Military Thought from Washington to Marshall* (Columbia University Press, New York, 1962), pp. 77–78, 107–108, 127–129, 138, 139–140, 144–149, 156, 222–224, 240–241, 248–250; also, Samuel P. Huntington, *The Soldier and the State* (Belknap Press, Harvard University, Cambridge, 1958), pp. 151–162, 193–373; and Paul Hammond, *Organizing for Defense: The American Military Establishment in the Twentieth Century* (Princeton University Press, Princeton, 1961), pp. 165–179, 182–185; also, Morris Janowitz, *The Professional Soldier: A Social and Political Portrait* (Glencoe Free Press, 1960). For a rather typical British criticism of Marshall's and Eisenhower's lack of strategic insight and political ingenuousness, see Wilmot, *The Struggle for Europe*, pp. 454–455, 715–716. The acerbic quotation is from Fuller, *The Second World War*, p. 361.

169

[3] Eisenhower, *Crusade in Europe*, pp. 419–427; Pogue, *op. cit.*, pp. 441–447; Ehrman, *op. cit.*, pp. 131–146; Montgomery, *Memoirs*, pp. 296–297. Also, based on letter from Montgomery to the author, June 19, 1963.

[4] Eisenhower, *Crusade in Europe*, pp. 386, 418–420; Bradley, *op. cit.*, pp. 445–447, 475, 494–495, 535.

[5] Harry C. Butcher, *My Three Years with Eisenhower; The Personal Diary of Captain Harry C. Butcher, U.S.N.R., Naval Aide to General Eisenhower, 1942–1945* (Simon and Schuster, New York, 1946), pp. 220, 287–288, 450 (hereafter cited as Butcher, *My Three Years with Eisenhower*); Bradley, *op. cit.*, pp. 206–207; Pogue, *op. cit.*, pp. 35, 289–290; Montgomery, *op. cit.*, pp. 483–484; Bryant, *op. cit.*, pp. 93–94, 150–154, 189–191, 391–398; Churchill, *op. cit.*, p. 468; Hastings Lionel Ismay, *The Memoirs of General Lord Ismay, K. G.* (Heineman, London, 1960), pp. 258–259, 263, 313–314, 357 (hereafter referred to as Ismay, *Memoirs*). For an analysis of Eisenhower's complex personality and his concern with moral and spiritual values as President, see Emmet John Hughes, *The Ordeal of Power: A Political Memoir of the Eisenhower Years* (Atheneum, New York, 1963); Eisenhower, *Crusade in Europe*, pp. 482–484.

[6] Eisenhower, *Crusade in Europe*, pp. 392–394, 404–406, 417–418, 428–430, 433; Smith, *Eisenhower's Six Great Decisions*, pp. 186–201.

[7] Eisenhower, *Crusade in Europe*, pp. 419–427; also based on letter from Eisenhower to the author, March 19, 1963.

[8] Pogue, *op. cit.*, pp. 407–416; 441–448, 468–469, 503–509.

[9] Letters from Eisenhower to the author, Oct. 31, 1962, and Mar. 19, 1963.

[10] Feis, *op. cit.*, pp. 610–611, 621–626, 633–634; Churchill, *op. cit.*, pp. 397–401, 429–445, 486–498; Pogue,

op. cit., pp. 468–469, 503–508; Ehrman, *op. cit.*, pp. 151–161.

[11] *Ibid.*, Eisenhower's, Churchill's and the American Joint Chiefs of Staff's views are all found in the works cited immediately above.

[12] Pogue, *op. cit.*, p. 435; Bryant, *op. cit.*, p. 444; Ehrman, *op. cit.*, pp. 133–134; letter to the author from a British military intelligence expert who must remain anonymous, March 7, 1962.

[13] Letters from British military intelligence experts to the author. The gentlemen must remain anonymous, March 7, 1962, May 3, 1962; Ehrman, *op. cit.*, p. 134; Frischauer, *The Rise and Fall of Hermann Goering*, pp. 252–253.

[14] Eisenhower, *Crusade in Europe*, pp. 417–418.

[15] Feis, *op. cit.*, pp. 583–596; Churchill, *op. cit.*, pp. 378–389; Ehrman, *op. cit.*, pp. 122–128.

[16] *Ibid.*; also, Farago, *Burn After Reading*, pp. 273–274.

CHAPTER 7

[1] Reitlinger, *The SS, Alibi of a Nation*, pp. 419–421; The New York *Times*, April 5, 1945, 1:3; Fraenkel, *Doctor Goebbels*, pp. 266–268; Rudolf Semmler, *Goebbels, The Man Next to Hitler*, pp. 187–193; Hugh Trevor-Roper, ed., *The Bormann Letters: The Private Correspondence Between Martin Bormann and His Wife from January, 1943, to April, 1945* (Weidenfeld and Nicolson, London, 1954), pp. 191, 196 (hereafter referred to as Trevor-Roper, *The Bormann Letters*).

[2] Von Hengl, *Report on the Fortress*, pp. 1–6; Marcinkiewicz, *Report*, pp. 5–10; Jacob, *Report on the Alpine Redoubt*, pp. 1–2.

[3] Albert Kesselring, *A Soldier's Record* (Morrow, New York, 1954), pp. 327–333 (hereafter cited as Kes-

selring, *A Soldier's Record*); Franz Halder, *Hitler as Warlord* (Putnam, London, 1950), pp. 68–69.

[4] Halder, *op. cit.*, pp. 68–69; letter to the author from Siegfried Westphal, Oct. 26, 1962; Kesselring, *op. cit.*, pp. 327–334; letter from Gunther Blumentritt to the author, Nov. 19, 1962. Blumentritt, fighting in the north against Montgomery, only heard rumors of an *Alpenfestung* in April, 1945.

[5] Kesselring, *op. cit.*, pp. 327–334.

[6] *Ibid.*

[7] Joachim Joesten, *European Reports, Hitler's Alpine Redoubt* (privately printed, New York, 1945), pp. 1–27 (hereafter cited as Joesten, *Hitler's Alpine Redoubt*); The New York *Times*, April 8, 1945, Sec. E3: 3–5. For an excellent pictorial presentation of the Redoubt in the popular mass media, see the relief map of the *Alpenfestung* in *Life* magazine (Chicago), April 9, 1945, pp. 38–39. During the month of April, practically all the national news weeklies such as *Time* and *Newsweek* repeatedly carried stories on the National Redoubt, but the accounts almost always were based upon information taken from articles in the New York *Times*.

[8] Smith, *Eisenhower's Six Great Decisions*, pp. 188–197.

[9] Letters to the author from Allen Dulles, Feb. 28, 1962, and Jan. 21, 1963; OSS Report, Seventh Army, April, 1945, cited in Lasky, *Field Notes* (OCMH files), pp. 6–7.

[10] Pogue, *The Supreme Command*, p. 435: sentiment within the OSS based on letters to the author from Professors Franklin L. Lord of Harvard, Dec. 12, 1962, Eugene Anderson of the University of California at Los Angeles, Oct. 24, 1962, and Carl E. Schorske of the University of California at Berkeley, October 30, 1962.

[11] Eisenhower, *Crusade in Europe*, pp. 430–431; Bradley, *A Soldier's Story*, pp. 530–546; Pogue, *op. cit.*,

pp. 444–447; William D. Leahy, *I Was There: the Personal Story of the Chief of Staff to Presidents Roosevelt and Truman Based on His Notes and Diaries Made at the Time* (Whittlesey House, New York, 1950), pp. 350–351 (hereafter referred to as Leahy, *I Was There*).

[12] Eisenhower, *Crusade in Europe*, pp. 419–431; Pogue, *op. cit.*, pp. 444–449.

[13] The directive, one sent to the Military Missions in Moscow, was quoted in Ehrman, *Grand Strategy*, VI, 145–148; Jean de Lattre de Tassigny, *The History of the French First Army* (G. Allen and Unwin, London, 1952), p. 482 (hereafter cited as de Tassigny, *The French First Army*). Also, Reuben E. Jenkins, "The Battle of the German National Redoubt," *Military Review*, XXVI (1947), 16; Allen, *Lucky Forward*, p. 378; William East and William Gleason, *The 409th Infantry in World War II* (Infantry Journal Press, Washington, 1947), pp. 136, 143 (hereafter cited as East and Gleason, *The 409th Infantry*).

[14] Churchill, *Triumph and Tragedy*, pp. 437–445; Ehrman, *op. cit.*, pp. 148–149.

[15] SHAEF G-2, *Joint Intelligence Committee* files, cited in Pogue, *op. cit.*, p. 448; Smith, *Eisenhower's Six Great Decisions*, pp. 176–177, 188–190, 196–197; de Tassigny, *op. cit.*, p. 482; *Allied Forces Headquarters, G-2 Intelligence Summary No. 15*, 17 April 1945, cited in Lasky, *Field Notes*, p. 7 (OCMH files). *SHAEF Weekly Intelligence Summary*, No. 57, 22 April 1945, cited in Lasky, *op. cit.*, p. 8.

[16] Third Army G-2 Information Bulletin No. 45, *circa* 15 April 1945, cited in Lasky, *op. cit.*, p. 9; Clinger, et al., *The History of the Seventy-first Infantry Division*, p. 70; The New York *Times*, April 16, 1945, 15:2–4.

[17] Pogue, *op. cit.*, pp. 448–469; The New York *Times*, April 17, 1945, 5:2.

CHAPTER 8

[1] Reiss, *Joseph Goebbels*, pp. 335–337; Trevor-Roper, *The Last Days of Hitler*, pp. 106–142; Reitlinger, *The SS, Alibi of a Nation*, p. 429; Willi Frischauer, *Himmler, The Evil Genius of the Third Reich* (Odhams, London, 1953), pp. 243–244 (hereafter referred to as Frischauer, *Himmler, The Evil Genius*); Manvell and Fraenkel, *Doctor Goebbels* (Simon and Schuster, New York, 1962), pp. 261–262, 272–279; Frischauer, *The Rise and Fall of Hermann Goering*, p. 253.

[2] *Ibid.* The information is found in all the sources cited immediately above.

[3] Trevor-Roper, *The Last Days of Hitler*, pp. 113–115.

[4] Reitlinger, *op. cit.*, pp. 415–437; Trevor-Roper, *The Last Days of Hitler*, pp. 115–116.

[5] Trevor-Roper, *The Last Days of Hitler*, pp. 116–120, 183–186, 212–213; Manvell and Fraenkel, *op. cit.*, pp. 268–273.

[6] Trevor-Roper, *The Last Days of Hitler*, pp. 123–142.

[7] Reitlinger, *op. cit.*, pp. 419–422; Feis, *Churchill, Roosevelt, Stalin*, pp. 583–596; Farago, *Burn After Reading*, pp. 273–274.

[8] Kesselring, *op. cit.*, pp. 327–333.

[9] *Ibid.*; Pogue, *op. cit.*, pp. 471–474.

[10] Letters from Ferdinand Schoerner to the author, Jan. 5, 1963, Jan. 23, 1963, and Mar. 17, 1963; Aschenauer, *Der Fall Schoerner*, pp. 82–90.

[11] Letter from Ferdinand Schoerner to the author, Jan. 23, 1963; Trevor-Roper, *The Last Days of Hitler*, pp. 142–195, 207–212.

[12] Aschenauer, *op. cit.*, pp. 82–90; Eisenhower, *Crusade in Europe*, p. 420.

[13] Von Hengl, *Report on the Fortress*, pp. 1–3; Mar-

cinkiewicz, *Report*, p. 13; Jacob, *Report on the Alpine Redoubt*, p. 2.

[14] Von Hengl, *op. cit.*, pp. 2–4.

[15] *Ibid.*, pp. 4–8; Marcinkiewicz, *op. cit.*, pp. 10, 12–15; SS General and General of the Field SS and Police Otto Hoffmann, *The Alpine Fortress* (Zuffenhausen, 13 May 1946, OCMH files), pp. 1–4 (hereafter cited as Hoffmann, *The Alpine Fortress*). For an excellent pictorial presentation of the Bavarian chaos in April and May, see *Life* magazine (Chicago), May 14, 1945, pp. 28–39, 103–110.

CHAPTER 9

[1] Butcher, *My Three Years with Eisenhower*, pp. 809–815. Butcher, as far as the author is able to tell, kept the only record of this particular off-the-record press conference.

[2] *Ibid.*

[3] The New York *Times*, April 22, 1945, 1:5, 7:5–8.

[4] *SHAEF Weekly Intelligence Summary, No. 57*, 22 April 1945, cited in Lasky, *Field Notes* (OCMH files), pp. 7–8; Patton, *War as I Knew It*, p. 309.

[5] Bradley, *op. cit.*, pp. 462, 536–537. Bradley commented that "most G-2's" were often pessimistic and alarmist. With close to a million men under his command, he found it impossible to read the intelligence reports of subordinate units, and so he had to depend upon his own G-2 and army commanders to keep him informed of the enemy's capabilities. This comment was made in appraisal of what he felt went wrong in regard to foreknowledge of the German Ardennes attack.

[6] *Ibid.*

[7] The New York *Times*, April 24, 1945, 1:3–4, 3:2–5, April 25, 1945, 1:6, 4:2, April 26, 1945, 14:2–3, April 28, 1945, 4:1–4; also Bradley, *op. cit.*, pp. 536–537.

[8] Feis *op. cit.*, pp. 583–596; Farago, *Burn After Read-*

175

ing, pp. 273–275; Ehrman, *op. cit.*, pp. 122–128; Reitlinger *op. cit.*, pp. 421–422.

CHAPTER 10

[1] *The Seventh Army United States Army in France and Germany 1944–1945: Report of Operations* (Heidelberg; 1946), III, 817–830 (hereafter cited as Seventh Army, *Report of Operations*).

[2] Third Army, *After Action Report, 1 August 1944 –9 May 1945* (printed in Europe, 1945), I, 352, 373–394; *ibid*, II, 44–49 (hereafter referred to as Third Army, *After Action Report*).

[3] Eugen Kogon, *The Theory and Practice of Hell: the German Concentration Camps and the System Behind Them* (Berkeley Publishing Corp., New York, 1960), pp. 228–234 (hereafter referred to as Kogon, *The Theory and Practice of Hell*).

[4] Pearson, *En Route to the Redoubt*, III, 86–87; Kogen, *op. cit.*, p. 275.

[5] Kogon, *op. cit.*, pp. 276–284; Seventh Army, *Report of Operations*, III, 831–832.

[6] Lasky, *op. cit.*, pp. 10–48; The New York *Times*, April 29, 1945, 1:3, 10:1–5; Hoffmann, *op. cit.*, p. 2; *I.M.T.*, IX, 194; Von Hengl, *op. cit.*, pp. 3–4.

[7] Von Hengl, *op. cit.*, pp. 8–9.

[8] Churchill, *op. cit.*, pp. 437–445; Ehrman, *op. cit.*, pp. 147–161; Pogue, *op. cit.*, pp. 451–456, 461–469.

[9] Pogue, *op. cit.*, p. 468.

[10] Feis, *op. cit.*, pp. 609–612; Pogue, *op. cit.*, pp. 468–469; Ehrman, *op. cit.*, pp. 155–163.

[11] *Ibid*. All the sources cited above bear on this incident. See Wilmot, *The Struggle for Europe*, pp. 705–706.

[12] Pogue, *op. cit.*, pp. 468–469; Ehrman, *op. cit.*, p. 160.

[13] Pogue, *op. cit.*, pp. 503–508.

[14] Jenkins, *loc. cit.*, pp. 22–25 .

[15] *Ibid;* also, Georges Blond, *The Death of Hitler's Germany* (New York, 1954), p. 232.

[16] Charles Foley, *Commando Extraordinary* (Longmans, Green, New York, 1954), pp. 148–151.

[17] Ronald Seth, *Anatomy of Spying: The Spy and His Techniques from Ancient Rome to the U-2* (E. P. Dutton, New York, 1963), pp. 247–250.

[18] Lasky, *op. cit*, pp. 11–20.

[19] Report of the G-3, *Forty-second Infantry Division*, 9 May 1945 (OCMH files); Pogue, *op. cit.*, pp. 478–494.

[20] Jenkins, *loc. cit.*, pp. 25–26; Pogue, *op. cit.*, pp. 482–483.

[21] Pogue, *op. cit.*, p. 483; Pearson, *Enroute to the Redoubt*, III, 214, 226–231.

[22] Pearson, *loc. cit.*, pp. 226–231.

[23] *Life* magazine (Chicago), May 28, 1945, pp. 30–31; Pogue, *op. cit.*, p. 348; also, Adolf Galland, *The First and the Last: The Rise and Fall of the German Fighter Forces, 1938–1945* (Holt, Rinehart and Winston, Inc., New York, 1954), pp. 347–360.

[24] Reitlinger, *op. cit.*, pp. 440–446.

[25] *Ibid.*, pp. 446–448.

[26] *Ibid.*, pp. 448–449.

CHAPTER 11

[1] Eisenhower, *Report of the Supreme Commander*, pp. 112–116.

[2] Feis, *Churchill, Roosevelt, Stalin*, pp. 611–612; Pogue, *The Supreme Command*, pp. 468–469.

[3] Feis, *op. cit.*, pp. 599–600, 636–641; Pogue, *op. cit.*, p. 495.

[4] *Supra*, pp. 72–77, 98–107, 166.

[5] For an outspoken commentary about these failures, see Esposito, *The West Point Atlas of American Wars*, II, text accompanying Map 72.

[6] S. L. A. Marshall, *Men Against Fire: the Problem of Battle Command in Future War* (Appolo edition, Morrow, New York, 1947), p. 108 (hereafter cited as Marshall, *Men Against Fire*).

[7] Pogue, *op. cit.*, pp. 359–404; Ehrman, *Grand Strategy*, VI, 64–76.

[8] Letter from Eisenhower to the author, Oct. 31, 1962.

[9] Eisenhower, *Crusade in Europe*, pp. 34–36, 142–143, 150–158; Pogue, *op. cit.*, pp. 71–72; Ladislas Farago, *War of Wits: the Anatomy of Espionage and Intelligence* (Funk & Wagnalls, New York, 1954), pp. 37–39 (hereafter referred to as Farago, *War of Wits*). Also, Farago, *Burn After Reading*, pp. 242–244.

[10] Pogue, *op. cit.*, pp. 71–73.

[11] General information on British wartime intelligence practices come from acknowledged experts who must remain anonymous for official as well as personal reasons. The reader must take the author's guarantee that their observations are backed by a wealth of experience. Criticism of American intelligence work during World War II is to be found in Farago, *Burn After Reading*, pp. 188–221, 242–302; Eisenhower, *Crusade in Europe*, pp. 34–36; also, Roberta Wohlstetter, *Pearl Harbor: Warning and Decision* (Stanford University Press, Palo Alto, California, 1962).

[12] *Ibid.*

[13] *Ibid.*

[14] Pogue, *op. cit.*, p. 72.

[15] *Ibid.* See also, Bradley, *A Soldier's Story*, pp. 462–464.

[16] Third Army, *After Action Report*, II, 54.

[17] Twelfth Army Group, *Report of Operations*, III, 116–120.

[18] Letter from former OSS official to the author, Nov. 23, 1962. The source must remain anonymous.

Biographical Notes

In assembling material for this book, the author was
faced by a special problem: some of the information
came from still-classified sources and if it was to be
quoted directly, the manuscript had to be submitted to
various agencies within the United States Army for
clearance. Furthermore, all notes had to be left in the
National Archives, World War II division, in Alexandria, Virginia, while the author's home and professional
duties were in California. Also there was the risk that
some anonymous reviewer would deny clearance for
reasons known only to himself.

To circumvent this problem, the author used as much
declassified primary source material as possible and
then relied on excellent secondary sources whose classi-

fied information had already been cleared by the Department of the Army. The author, however, also obtained security clearance. During a trip to Washington, D.C., he personally studied all the classified records available on the *Alpenfestung* and also those cited in the secondary sources to double-check facts, to ferret out new information, and to test interpretations. Admittedly, all the strange details of the National Redoubt may not as yet have come to light nor may they ever, but this account is as honest, thorough, and accurate a one as the writer could fashion.

PRIMARY SOURCES

The most important primary sources that pertain to the National Redoubt are those documents from the files of the Supreme Headquarters, Allied Expeditionary Force, and the Office, Chief of Military History (OCMH). The classified SHAEF files examined by the author contain various of the separate records of the special staff divisions within SHAEF such as *G-2 Intelligence Summaries*, *Joint Intelligence Committee* papers, *Counter Intelligence Sub-Division Reports*, *Office of Strategic Services Research and Analysis Reports*, *Prisoner of War Interrogation Reports*, *Prisoner of War Intelligence Bulletins*, *Mobile Field Unit Interrogation Reports*, *G-3 Operations Files*, and four fascinating volumes of the SHAEF *In and Out Cable Logs* for 1945. The messages in the cable logs were examined daily by Eisenhower and the volumes contain paraphrases of all the cables addressed to Eisenhower and those sent out in his name. Many have his penciled comments in the margin.

Other files, largely declassified, which were examined came primarily from OCMH records and included: a *G-2 Report on the National Redoubt* from the *Sixth Army Group File*, which divulges the information that the French army intelligence sections swallowed the Redoubt fantasia no less than their American comrades; the credulous March 25, 1945, *Seventh Army G-2 Study on the German National Redoubt and Related Documents;* and the March 21, 1945, Headquarters, Twelfth Army Group, *Reorientation of Strategy*, Appendix A, *G-2 Report on the Redoubt.*

The OCMH files also produced several very important interrogations of German officers or officials who, in one way or another, were directly connected with the *Alpenfestung.* The most important of these interviews are Lieutenant General Georg Ritter von Hengl's *Report on the Alpine Fortress* (April, 1946, MS No. B-459, OCMH), Lieutenant General Alfred Jacob's *Report Concerning the German Alpine Redoubt* (Allendorf, 1946, MS No. B-188, OCMH), Brigadier General Marcinkiewicz' *Report on the Alpenfestung* (Allendorf, June, 1946, MS No. B-187, OCMH), and Franz Hofer's *Alpenstallung-Alpenfestung* (MSS No. 457, OCMH).

The first three interrogation accounts are extremely valuable, for the officers involved were not only intelligent but were highly proficient in their respective

181

fields. Von Hengl was a mountain expert, while Jacob
and Marcinkiewicz were engineers. Hofer's account is
no less valuable, though from a political point of view.
Interestingly enough, it is only from the Germans that
we get a resumé of the original American State Department report on the Redoubt sent from Switzerland. The State Department today refers inquiries
about that report to the Department of the Army
which, in turn, advises the correspondent to go to the
Office, Chief of Military History. Hofer's version of
the American report is the only one that this author
has been able to find. It appears, however, that Hofer's
story was reasonably well known in certain Nazi
circles, for Wilhelm Hoettl makes reference to the
same set of circumstances by which the idea of an
Alpenfestung was born in Germany. To the best of
the writer's knowledge, Hoettl never has had access
to the files of the OCMH or read Hofer's interrogation
report.

Of less value than the OCMH files, is SS General
Otto Hoffmann's *The Alpine Fortress* (Zuffenhausen,
13 May 1946, OCMH). Hoffmann's report is less
valuable only in regard to the technical details of the
Alpenfestung. He literally knew nothing about it. The
document, however, is important in its account of the
morale breakdown of the populace and the troops
within the Redoubt.

Finally, there are two other sources which are not
from the OCMH files. One is the *Trial of Major War
Criminals Before the International Military Tribunal*

182

(Nuremberg, 1948), and the OSS, Research and Analysis Branch, R and A No. 232, *South Germany: An Analysis of the Political and Social Organization, the Communications, Economic Controls, Agriculture and Food Supply, Mineral Resources, Manufacturing and Transportation Facilities of South Germany* (Washington, 1944). Both of these are in the Hoover Institute on War, Revolution and Peace at Stanford University. The Institute also housed the bulk of the secondary sources used by the author.

SECONDARY SOURCES

The amount of material available through secondary sources is tremendous. Commentaries follow on the most important ones for this story; the remainder are cited in the footnotes.

Two official reports are extremely important: *Report by the Supreme Commander to the Combined-Chiefs-of-Staff on the Operations in Europe of the Allied Expeditionary Force, 6 June 1944 to 8 May 1945* (Government Printing Office, Washington, 1945), and *The Winning of the War in Europe and the Pacific; Biennial Report of the Chief-of-Staff of the United States Army 1943 to 1954, to the Secretary of War, War Department* (Government Printing Office, Washington, 1945). An account of interest is Melvin Lasky's *Seventh Army—Field Notes on the Disintegration of the German Army* (Augsburg, 1945, unpublished MS, OCMH). This is really two tales in one: the delusion of the Redoubt and the revolt of Munich on March 28,

1945. His analysis of the Redoubt is not as detailed as his research on Munich's revolt, the latter a little-known story of the war that deserves more attention.

An indispensable secondary source is Forrest C. Pogue's *The Supreme Command: United States Army in World War II Series* (Office of the Chief of Military History, Department of the Army, Washington, D.C., 1954). Pogue's book, one of a detailed series, is excellent. He had unlimited access to most of the available sources including Eisenhower's personal file. Currently, he is at work on volumes on General of the Army George C. Marshall, wartime Chief of Staff. Pogue's style is undramatic in dealing with controversial topics, but his restraint is commendable. Many historians writing of war imply that they could have fought the campaigns better than the men who did. Pogue avoids this pitfall. If he has one fault, it is perhaps that he tends to gloss over the political naïveté of Marshall, Eisenhower, and Bradley. But his book is an outstanding one and the basic volume for anyone intent on reading the American version of how SHAEF was organized and administered under Eisenhower.

Other equally important books, most of which are memoirs, are Dwight D. Eisenhower, *Crusade in Europe* (Dolphin Paperback Co., New York, 1961); John Ehrman, *Grand Strategy* (H.M. Stationery Office, London, 1956), VI; Milton Shuman, *Defeat in the West* (E. P. Dutton, New York, 1948); Omar N. Bradley, *A Soldier's Story* (Holt, Rinehart and Winston, New York, 1951); George S. Patton, Jr., *War as I Knew It* (Houghton Mifflin, Boston, 1947); Lucien K. Truscott, Jr., *Command Decisions; A Personal History* (E. P. Dutton, New York, 1954); Mark Clark, *Calculated Risk* (Harper Bros., New York, 1950); Walter Bedell Smith, *Eisenhower's Six Great Decisions* (Longman's, New York, 1956); Arthur Bryant, *Triumph in the West, 1943–1946: Based on the Diaries and Autobiographical Notes of Field Marshal The Viscount Alanbrooke, K.G., O.M.* (Collins, London, 1959); Winston Churchill, *The Second World War: Triumph and Tragedy* (Bantam Paperback Books, New York, 1962), VI; Bernard L. Montgomery, *The Memoirs of Field Marshal The Viscount Montgomery of Alamein, K.G.* (World Publishing Co., New York and Cleveland, 1958); Major General Sir Francis de Guingand, *Operation Victory* (Charles Scribner's Sons, New York, 1947); Hastings Lionel Ismay; *The Memoirs of General Lord Ismay, K.G.* (Heineman, London, 1960); William D. Leahy, *I Was There; the Personal Story of the Chief of Staff to Presidents Roosevelt and Truman Based on His Notes and Diaries Made at the Time* (Whittlesey House, New York, 1950); Jean de Lattre Tassigny, *The History of the French First Army* (G. Allen and Unwin, London, 1952); Herbert Feis, *Churchill, Roosevelt, Stalin; The War They Waged and the Peace They Sought* (Princeton University Press, Princeton, N.J., 1957); and Harry C. Butcher, *My Three Years with Eisenhower; the Personal Diary of Captain Harry C. Butcher, U.S.N.R., Naval Aide to General Eisen-*

185

hower, 1942–1945 (Simon and Schuster, New York, 1946).

Eisenhower's book would be fundamental in assessing any aspect of the campaigns in Europe. What was written in 1948 closely follows what he felt during the war. In recent years, however, he has had a somewhat different viewpoint on some events and the effects of some wartime decisions.

Bradley's account, *A Soldier's Story*, is an extremely frank one, giving his version of many contentious events, especially those that involved Montgomery and himself. The book is marred somewhat for fussy scholars by its colloquial approach, but the contents are invaluable for the interested student. Much the same may be said of Patton's book. Mark Clark and Lucien Truscott's books concern the fighting in Italy. Both men, although they had their troubles with their British allies, sensed that the British concern with political ramifications arising from combat operations was a valid one. The styles of the books sometimes veer off in the direction of the high-school-student fullback recounting his gridiron exploits, but both also round out the picture of the confused and dreary Italian campaign.

Necessary books are Walter Bedell Smith's *Eisenhower's Six Great Decisions*, Harry Butcher's *My Three Years with Eisenhower*, and Admiral William Leahy's *I Was There*. Smith was Eisenhower's Chief of Staff at SHAEF and Butcher was the Supreme Commander's aide. Smith's book follows the record as it actually was and as it may be checked today from the SHAEF files. In regard to the Redoubt, there is no mistaking the fact that in the spring of 1945 Smith regarded the threat of an Alpine stronghold as a distinct one. Butcher's account of life at SHAEF is a piece of military social history. Its chief value lies in the fact that occasionally Butcher recorded incidents which are usually left out of official histories and memoirs. The off-the-record press conference of April 21, 1945, in which Smith evaluated the Redoubt is one such example.

Leahy's *I Was There* is one of the basic sources of the wartime decisions of the American Joint Chiefs of Staff. Pogue's volume dealing with Marshall's role, however, will undoubtedly throw further light on the part played by the Joint Chiefs.

Herbert Feis's book on *Churchill, Roosevelt and Stalin* is an excellent diplomatic history and one of a series written by the author dealing with the World War II period.

The British sources listed here all have one slight advantage over their American counterparts—the style of all of them is extremely literate. Churchill's importance and style hardly need commentary. Montgomery's and Ismay's styles are far from being as polished as the former Prime Minister's, though both men express themselves in a spritely but dignified fashion. Naturally, there is a wide variance between the ways in which Bradley and Montgomery viewed the same war. Montgomery, a more conservative soldier than

Bradley, was forced to work within a system whereby his civilian leaders kept tight control of the strategic and even the tactical moves of his army. Bradley noted this factor and was frank to admit that field commanders within the American army had more freedom of action without an accounting to Washington. Montgomery's main trouble, however, in regard to his American colleagues, seems to have been that his mannerisms infuriated them. Not deliberately tactless, he had an astounding self-confidence which was not tempered by any signs of personal humility. When one considers Eisenhower's job of making such diverse personalities as a Patton and a Montgomery fight the Germans rather than each other, it adds another dimension to his handling of the problem of command. Montgomery's troubles are well portrayed in his Chief of Staff's book, *Operation Victory*, by Major General Sir Francis de Guingand.

Ismay's chronicle really does not go into too much detail of the decision-making he saw during the war. His paragraphs on Eisenhower, however, are fascinating. Ismay was an avowed proponent of the Supreme Commander's conduct of the European campaign. By contrast, Lord Alanbrooke's portrayal of Eisenhower is that the American general was a charming amateur who needed constant guidance from his more experienced British comrades. The tone of the British Chief of the Imperial Staff's diaries is waspish, but this may be due to the fact that Alanbrooke was a desperately weary man during most of the war. Also, like many

Britons, Alanbrooke quite naturally resented the fact that from 1944 onward the Americans began to dominate the formulation of all policies. It was galling for the British to have fought virtually alone for four years and then have their responsibilities and experience count for little at victory's threshold.

John Ehrman's *Grand Strategy* is an excellently written volume in the British official historical series dealing with World War II. As one reads Pogue's *The Supreme Command*, it is vital also to read Ehrman, who has managed to include verbatim reports from cables, orders, memos, and various reports to which Pogue merely refers or paraphrases. The reader, if he will read both books concurrently, will be able to cross-check and decide which author presents the more accurate interpretation. Obviously, at times the advantage may shift from one writer to the other. Ehrman's book, no less than Pogue's, is a necessity for those interested in the European campaigns of the British and Americans.

Milton Shulman is an ex-major in the Canadian army who set about to write the story of the German army, relying mainly on German sources. The result is remarkable. His investigation left him disgusted with the professional German military and its essential immorality born of an apolitical tradition and an over-dependence upon form and discipline peculiar to its immediate caste. They were, Shulman feels, far from being supermen and omnipotent in their craft. The thesis of the book is that no army in modern times was

189

as badly and thoroughly defeated as Germany's between 1939–1945. Shulman detracts from his impressive narrative by a final chapter that becomes an anti-German, anti-Nazi polemic. Also, in that chapter, he blurs the essential difference between the old-line officer-corps product and the newer National Socialist. Except for that weakness, the book is first-rate.

The numbers of regimental, battalion, and divisional histories are almost infinite. The author has recorded in his footnotes all such accounts used. The quality, as might be expected, varies tremendously. Most are badly written and not all are as accurate as one might wish. They do, however, provide valuable color to finish off the portraits of various events. Of far more value to the historian are the *After Action Reports* of the principal army groups and armies involved. These histories, which are semiofficial, are prone to some of the same errors as the histories of lower units. They do, though, give an over-all, sweeping picture of the armies' operations. The author relied upon volume III of the Twelfth Army Group, *Report of Operations (Final After Action Report)* (printed in Europe, 1945), fourteen volumes; Sixth Army Group *Operations Report* (monthly mimeographed reports); Third Army, *After Action Report, 1 August 1944–9 May 1945* (printed in Europe, 1945), two volumes; *The Seventh United States Army in France and Germany 1944–1945: Report of Operations* (Heidelberg, 1946), three volumes.

Secondary source books about Hitler and Nazi Germany have been written in great numbers, too. Many historians and journalists have taken an intense interest in dissecting the macabre Third Reich, possibly because its evilness symbolizes so much of what is wrong with this unhappy century.

Alan L. C. Bullock, *Hitler; A Study in Tyranny* (Harper and Row, New York, 1952) is a superb history of the demented German leader. Definitive histories about Adolf Hitler perhaps are still to come, but until they do, Bullock's book will remain the prime one in its field. Another British historian, H. Trevor-Roper of Oxford, wrote a minor classic in *The Last Days of Hitler* (Macmillan, New York, 1947). He also edited *The Bormann Letters: The Private Correspondence Between Martin Bormann and His Wife from January, 1943, to April, 1945* (Weidenfeld and Nicolson, London, 1954). Perhaps no other books capture the insane atmosphere of the collapsing Nazi state as well as these two do. *The Last Days* is an accurate reconstruction of life in Hitler's bunker in Berlin as the Russians make their final conquest of the city. With the exception of Paul Josef Goebbels, Bormann, a little publicized Nazi, was perhaps the man closest to Hitler during the war years. Bormann's death in Berlin has been a subject of continuing mystery and from time to time stories crop up that he is living in Argentina today.

The Minister of Propaganda for the Third Reich was Goebbels and his remarkable career has been studied in three books: Roger Manvell and Heinrich Fraenkel, *Doctor Goebbels; His Life and Death* (Heineman, London, 1960); Curt Reiss, *Joseph Goeb-*

bels, A Biography (Doubleday, Garden City, N.Y., 1948), and Rudolf Semmler, *Goebbels, The Man Next to Hitler* (Westhouse, London, 1947). Goebbels was unquestionably the most intelligent and probably the ablest of the Nazi leaders. With the exception of Hitler himself, he was also the most nihilistic of the top Nazis. He desired the death of all of Germany rather than capitulation, and his murder of his own children and his subsequent suicide and that of his wife symbolized his philosophy. If, indeed, it may be dignified by such a title.

The books on Hermann Goering, so far, have not been quite as good as the ones on Hitler and Goebbels. Conceivably, this is because his was a more superficial personality and does not excite the researcher's curiosity. The best that have appeared are: Ewan Butler and Gordon Young, *Marshal Without Glory* (Hodders and Stoughton, London, 1951); Roger Manvell and Heinrich Fraenkel, *Goering* (Simon and Schuster, New York, 1962); and Willi Frischauer, *The Rise and Fall of Hermann Goering* (Houghton Mifflin, Boston, 1951).

One of the most provocative and intriguing books about Nazi Germany is Gerald Reitlinger's *The SS, Alibi of a Nation, 1922–1945* (Heineman, London, 1956). Reitlinger recounts the whole sordid history of the SS and its dreary leader, Heinrich Himmler, the erstwhile chicken farmer. Reitlinger did a monumental job of research in tracking down all the innumerable plots and political schisms within the elite organization.

The SS defies imagination. A book dealing solely with Himmler, is Willi Frischauer's *Himmler: The Evil Genius of The Third Reich* (Odhams, London, 1953).

Wilhelm Hoettl, who uses the pseudonym Walter Hagen was one of the many Austrians who seemed to infest the elite *Schutzstaffel* (SS). He was in the *Sicherheitsdienst* (SD or Security Service) where he served as a "scientific adviser" to the SD's political section and dealt with intelligence affairs. While much of his commentary upon German intelligence activities is illuminating, his words must be carefully weighed, for he has a tendency toward exaggeration and invention. He has written a few sensationalist-type books and articles upon his activities in the SS. What he has to say should be checked or verified from other sources. His claim that he talked to Dulles personally is one example of his ability to embroider facts. Dulles deliberately never met with Hoettl, although he knew who the Nazi intelligence officer was and, in fact, had an agent in touch with him. Hoettl's books and articles used by the author are as follows: Walter Hagen (pseud.) *Unternehmen Bernard; ein historischer Tatsachenbericht—uber die grosste Geldfalschungsaktion aller Zeiten* (Welsund Stornberg, Verlag Welsermuhl, 1955); and the English version of the same story which had appeared earlier, Wilhelm Hoettl, *Hitler's Paper Weapon* (R. Hart and Davis, London, 1945); Wilhelm Hoettl as told to Ladislas Farago, "I Was Hitler's Master Spy," *Argosy*, CCCXXXVII (1953). "Operation Bernhard" was a Nazi attempt to flood the British

193

and American markets with counterfeit pound and dollar notes.

Of great interest, especially because it is little known outside of Germany, is the defense of Field Marshal Ferdinand Schoerner by his lawyer in the trial for Schoerner's conduct during the war. The apologia is Rudolf Aschenauer's *Der Fall Schoerner; Eine Klarstellung* (privately printed, Munich, 1962). Schoerner distributed copies of his story to many former German army officers and he also sent one to the author after an exchange of correspondence.

In addition to Schoerner, the author also used four books written by German field marshals or high-ranking officers. Adolf Galland, *The First and the Last: The Rise and Fall of the German Fighter Forces, 1938–1945* (Holt, Rinehart and Winston, New York, 1954); Heinz Guderian, *Erinnerungen eines Soldaten* (K. Vowinckel, Heidelberg, 1951); Franz Halder, *Hitler As Warlord* (Putnam, London, 1950), and Albert Kesselring, *A Soldier's Record* (Morrow, New York, 1954).

As might be expected, comments from the "other side of the hill" are of great interest. There is an understandable tendency, however, for surviving professional German officers to blame Hitler for everything that went wrong and claim credit themselves for any successes. They cannot have it both ways, for many of the spectacular early victories were as much due to Hitler's imagination as the later defeats were products of his nihilism. It was he who saw the possibilities of

194

the Blitzkrieg when many professionals did not. It was he who elevated Guderian and Kesselring to their places of eminence partially because they possessed a verve he admired. When things went very wrong after 1942, Hitler could be blamed after any disastrous event because his notions of static defense were absurd in the face of reality. But also, as Forrest Pogue has noted, too many Germans have blamed their defeat not only on Hitler but also on the Western Allied preponderance of men and material. This, of course, disregards the fighting qualities of the conscript American soldier and his army. The German thesis is that without his excellent equipment, the GI would have been no soldier at all. The World War II GI is a baffling figure to the German, for he was most often only as good as he had to be to get the job done. He was amateurish on D-Day, but he prevailed; at first many GI's were terrified and ran in the Ardennes, but they also stood at Bastogne and then they all wearily marched back, pulverizing the German army in the process. The story in the Pacific was much the same. Furthermore, although the GI's possessed an abundance of equipment, it was not always as good as their German adversaries'. Much the same may be said of the British Tommy as well, although undeniably the British troops had been at war longer than the Americans and were thus true veterans, being better disciplined and more professional. But they had had to learn the hard way, too. The British, also, had a more direct stake in defeating Germany. The question concerning the American as a fighting man in World War II is not why did he fight so badly, but why, in view of his lack of emotional commitment to the war effort, did he fight so well? Often a German reviewing the war's military history ignores such factors.

Two excellent British accounts of the war, which are largely critical of American military and diplomatic policies, may be found in J. F. C. Fuller's *The Second World War, 1939–1945; A Strategical and Tactical History* (Duell, Sloan & Pearce, New York, 1949), and Chester Wilmot's *The Struggle for Europe* (Collins, London, 1952). Fuller's book is by a recognized military expert. Extreme conservatives in both England and the United States will appreciate his damnation of Franklin Roosevelt's wartime foreign policy or, rather, the lack of it. Wilmot, no military expert, was an extremely competent journalist. His book is opinionated, but well worth reading. Eisenhower is Wilmot's bumbling, if attractive, villain.

SPECIALIZED SUBJECTS

Books of a more specialized nature are: Georges Blond, *The Death of Hitler's Germany* (Macmillan, New York, 1954); Vincent J. Esposito, Jr. (ed.), *The West Point Atlas of American Wars* (Praeger, New York, 1959), two volumes; Charles Foley, *Commando Extraordinary* (Longmans, Green, London and New York, 1954); two books by Ladestas Farago, *Burn After Reading: The Espionage of World War II* (Walker and Co., New York, 1961), and *War of*

196

Wits: the Anatomy of Espionage and Intelligence
(Funk & Wagnalls, New York, 1954); Kent R. Green-
field, ed., *Command Decisions* (Harcourt, Brace, New
York, 1959); Eugen Kogon, *The Theory and Practice
of Hell: The German Concentration Camps and the
System Behind Them* (New Berkeley Medallion edi-
tion, Berkeley Publishing Corp., New York, 1960);
Jon Kimche, *Spying for Peace; General Guisan and
Swiss Neutrality* (Weidenfeld and Nicolson, London,
1962); S. L. A. Marshall, *Men Against Fire: The
Problem of Battle Command in Future War* (Appolo
edition, William Morrow and Co., New York, 1947).
An excellent article on the reduction of the Redoubt
is Reuben E. Jenkins', "The Battle of the German Na-
tional Redoubt—Planning Phase," *Military Review*,
XXVI (1946–1947).

Blond's journalistic account is written from the
French viewpoint. Esposito, a colonel at West Point,
has compiled a superlative two-volume set of detailed
American military campaign maps. His text is good,
too. Foley's book is a journalistic account of the SS
hero, Otto Skorzeny. Farago's books on espionage and
intelligence are interesting although, again, scholarly
purists will object to his journalistic style. Greenfield's
Command Decisions was prepared under the auspices
of the Office, Chief of Military History and includes a
variety of essays or monographs analyzing various
battles, strategic decisions, and campaigns of the Second World War. Kogon's book on the Nazi death
camps is a chilling one. His approach is almost that of

197

a sociologist and the horror of the tale is emphasized by his socio-scientific treatment of the subject. He was a German political prisoner in Buchenwald. Kimche's story concerns the building of the Swiss *national reduit* and the difficult task that nation had to maintain its neutrality and integrity at key times during the war. Marshall is the well-known military editor for the Detroit *News* and has written a series of books dealing with Americans' reactions under combat conditions. Jenkins, an American general, wrote a good account of the Redoubt's reduction.

PERSONAL LETTERS

The author can never thank adequately the soldiers and civilians of both sides who corresponded at length with him about the tale of the National Redoubt. I am unable to list the names of several former key intelligence personnel in the United States and Great Britain whose stories, advice, and general comments were invaluable. Allen Dulles, however, was one former intelligence expert who was extremely generous. Other former OSS personnel, now in the academic world, who were most helpful in their commentaries included, Professor Eugene Anderson of the University of California at Los Angeles, Franklin Ford of Harvard University, and Carl E. Schorske of the University of California at Berkeley.

Generals Dwight D. Eisenhower and Omar N. Bradley were exceptionally gracious in responding to a series of detailed letters asking them questions concerning the Redoubt. No less gracious than the Americans was Field Marshal the Viscount Montgomery of Alamein, K.G., who took the trouble to write his replies in his own hand. Sadly, the death of Field Marshal the Viscount Alanbrooke, K.G., O.M., during the writing of this book, prevented any personal communication between the author and that excellent British soldier. His editor and biographer, Sir Arthur Bryant, however, kindly answered pertinent queries addressed to him about the late Lord Alanbrooke.

Former German officers also were extremely kind in replying to questions put to them by the author. These officers included: General Gunther Blummentritt, whose main area of operations at the war's end was against Montgomery's Twenty-first Army Group; Lieutenant General Hans Speidel, formerly Chief of Staff to the legendary "Desert Fox," Erwin Rommel, and an officer who was under arrest by the Nazis from the fall of 1944 until the surrender in May, 1945; Lieutenant General Siegfried Westphal, Chief of Staff to Field Marshals Gerd von Rundstedt and Albert Kesselring during the last months of the war; and Field Marshal Ferdinand Schoerner, the last designated "Commander" of the *Alpenfestung* and the commander of the German army Group Center fighting so desperately in the Sudetenland at the time of the German surrender.

Index

207

United States (*Continued*)
 intelligence, 89–90, 110, 113, 143–49, 150–57, 175
 State Dept., 18–19, 182
 War Dept., 12
 See also Western Allies
United States Army. *See by designation*
United States Army Infantry Divisions:
 42nd, 116, 125
 45th, 112, 116
 71st, 94
 80th, 114
 88th, 5–8
 103rd, 112–13

Vienna, 75, 97
Vltava River, 119
Von Hengl, Georg Ritter, 103–107, 109, 117, 182
Von Loeb, Wilhelm Ritter, 127
Von Rundstedt, Gerd, 13, 63, 127
Von Vietinghoff, Heinrich Gottfried, 58, 79, 100, 111
Von Westrop, Countess Gisela, 127

Waffen SS, 17
Waibel, Max, 33–35

Wehrmacht, 110
Weimar Republic, 115
Weltwoche, 94
Werewolves, 28–29, 53, 83, 93n, 129, 153
West German Federal Republic, 102n, 124n
Western Allies, 11f, 22, 42, 60
 and Berlin, 48–49
 and Himmler's negotiations, 56–57, 99
 and Russians, 20, 39–40, 42, 79–80, 86–87, 110, 136
 split between, 69–71
 See also Press; SHAEF
Westphal, Siegfried, 86
Wilmot, Chester, 120–21
Winter, August, 101, 103, 109
Wolff, Karl:
 and German surrender in Italy, 32–41 *passim*, 79–80, 99, 138, 156
 and Kaltenbrunner, 58ff, 83, 99–100, 111
 mentioned, 9, 151

Yugoslavia, 118

Zimmer, Guido, 32–33
Zhukov, Marshal, 47

208

REDOUBT CENTER